MONEY
MAKER

Dear Nic,

Thank you for believing in me &
making Million Pound Pawn! This
book wouldn't exist if it hadn't
been for that show!

Sending Best Wishes

Dan

MONEY MAKER

UNLOCK YOUR MONEY-MAKING POTENTIAL

Dan Hatfield

Joff Hatfield-Powell

First published in Great Britain in 2024 by Hodder Catalyst
An imprint of Hodder & Stoughton Limited
An Hachette UK company

1

Design and illustrations by Goldust Design.
Images on pages 1, 3, 5, 19, 24, 40, 78, 93, 96, 97, 128, 113, 143,
159, 175, 199, 229, 258, 270 and 272: © Shutterstock. Image on
page 247: used with permission from Sheffield Assay Office.

A CIP catalogue record for this title is available
from the British Library

Hardback ISBN 978 1 399 73043 3
ebook ISBN 978 1 399 73044 0
Audiobook ISBN 978 1 399 73045 7

Typeset in Charter by Goldust Design

Printed and bound in Great Britain by Clays Ltd, Elcograf S.p.A.

Hodder & Stoughton policy is to use papers that are natural,
renewable and recyclable products and made from wood grown
in sustainable forests. The logging and manufacturing processes
are expected to conform to the environmental
regulations of the country of origin.

Hodder Catalyst
Hodder & Stoughton Limited
Carmelite House
50 Victoria Embankment
London EC4Y 0DZ

www.hoddercatalyst.co.uk

CONTENTS

1. Introducing You to Your Bubble

Your bubble is you and the sphere you inhabit – your home, your work, your life, your possessions, your time. Once you understand what you have, you can begin to learn how your bubble can make you money in a sustainable way.

2. The Great Big Life Audit

Do you know how much you currently spend and what you need to maintain the lifestyle you are accustomed to? We'll do a personal profit and loss sheet and debunk any fear around this simple financial aid. Then we'll investigate your SWOT – your strengths, weaknesses, opportunities and threats.

3. The Cash Calendar

Make a cash calendar so that at the beginning of each month you can assess the cost of your lifestyle – both necessities and things you choose to spend your cash on. We'll look at how much extra money you can make each month. You'll also look at how to raise more capital to fund big life moments – weddings/holidays/cars/childcare/university, etc.

11. Moonlight for Money

Your spare time could make you serious cash from the comfort of your own home. A third of under 30-year-olds have a side hustle to bolster their income and we could all earn a lot more if we adapted their perspective. We'll look at how extra-curricular activities and your hobbies could not only supplement your income but put some proper dough in your hands.

12. Car Boot for Extra Loot

There are up to 30,000 car boot sales across the UK each year raking in a whopping £1.5 billion. They are a surefire and sustainable way to clear your home and pocket the profit. Learn how best to car boot as well as the top tricks for getting the best price for your possessions.

13. Upcycle to Up-sell

The worldwide market of upcycling is worth £160 billion per year. Whether it's a simple lick of paint or giving a new purpose to an old, unused item, there is money to be made from upcycling. Find out how to identify what you could do with unwanted items around your home, how much money they could make you and where to sell them on.

14. Festive Funds

Christmas is not only the season for giving; it can be a very lucrative time of year. Over the festive period a lot of people are time-poor, which is where you can cash in. Whether decorating people's homes, making Christmas cards or even becoming Santa for the local shopping parade.

To all of those who have borrowed money
from us in the past... We hope this book
will help you pay us back!

INTRODUCING YOU TO YOUR BUBBLE

Whilst there are endless books that can teach you how to save money, *Money Maker* is going to help put more pounds in your pocket in the first place, without having to sacrifice the things in life you love.

Let's face it, regardless of the financial status of the world, one thing is constant: we can always benefit from some extra cash in our accounts. Life comes at a premium and we all strive to have the best for ourselves and our family. So I have always wondered why there isn't a book on the market to teach you how to make money. I'm not talking about making you the next Bill Gates or Oprah Winfrey – though if you have their brains and tenacity, good for you. I'm talking about enabling you to release the cash potential you have all around you which you don't even realise.

There is no witchcraft within this book – it is a resource that I hope is accessible and relatable to all. Within each chapter, we will delve into key areas of your life and help you to realise the value within it. Whatever age or stage of life you are at, I am going to teach you how to generate more cash whilst having fun along the way. **Make sure you follow me on Instagram for even more top tips and advice @DanHatfieldPawn.**

Did you know that, as a nation, we have an estimated £48 billion of unwanted goods just lying around, gathering dust? Once you've taken a moment to pick your jaw up off the floor, I'm going to show you ways to release those funds into your bank balance.

Whether tapping into skills that could make you money, renting out possessions to set up a steady additional income or finding fun new hobbies you can get paid to do, *Money Maker* will help you to raise the extra funds you want for whatever reason. It might be an unexpected bill, a dream family holiday or an expensive time of year, but whatever the reason, this book is the one-stop shop where you can learn the practical tips and tricks you need to turn yourself, your home, technology, spare time and so much more into hard cash.

We all have the potential to earn more, but in order to understand how, we first need to explore what I call our 'bubble'. Once you know what's in your bubble, you'll know how best to exploit it and fast become a 'bubble entre-preneur' – which is my fancy way of saying making more money from your skills and belongings.

So, what is a bubble? Putting it in its simplest form, it's basically your life. The physical form of you, the belongings you own and the incredible skills you may not even know you have. No bubble is the same, so the world is full of diverse and unique bubbles ready to be popped to expand their profit-making potential.

To better understand your bubble, I want you to delve deep

inside your mind. Consider the activities you like doing and the ones you dislike doing. Then walk around your home and room-by-room identify what you could monetise, either by making use of that item as a skill you can be hired for, or selecting the items you can sell or rent. For instance, I enjoy dog walking but dislike cleaning. Create your own bubble diagram to highlight all your likes, dislikes, assets and belongings.

Now that we know what is in your bubble, we can look at how we can turn your assets into cash, making you a bubble entrepreneur in no time at all.

What I am about to teach you isn't rocket science; you don't need a degree to understand my methods, and the only thing you'll need to invest is your time. By reading my book, the least you'll learn is how to turn some pennies into pounds, but with the right level of patience and commitment, *Money Maker* could have you maximising your money-making potential and living a life of financial satisfaction. If you follow some of the principles explained here, this book will put those extra pounds into your pocket.

I do have to make you aware that, whilst I am very proud of what I have learnt over my career, this book is my personal advice from my experiences. I am not offering any legal, tax, consumer rights, health and safety and/or regulatory advice. It is each reader's responsibility to ensure they are following the law and any other regulations that may impact and affect their personal situation when carrying out any activity discussed here. I truly believe everyone has the ability to financially thrive with this book, so do make sure to check how your success may affect your personal tax liability.

With that settled, let's start looking at how we can all make some more money!

THE GREAT BIG LIFE AUDIT

We're going to have to be honest with each other if I am going to successfully help you unleash your money-making potential. So, let's speak frankly. We need to look at the big picture – the good, the bad and the downright ugly of your current finances. We're going to take an overview of your life, your current financial situation, the financial drains you face and what assets you have (this is why you created your bubble diagram in Chapter 1).

To turn you into a bubble entrepreneur, I need this honest analysis to form the foundations of what you need to change to better your financial future. So, what is working in your life and what isn't? I need you to look at what finances you bring in and then what is taken out. I need to understand how you are currently surviving financially so that I can help you to thrive financially.

Of course, you could cut costs and look at various ways to reduce your outgoings by having or doing less, but that all gets a bit gloomy to be honest, and what I want to do is help you to learn what you need to do it order to have the money for a life that makes you happy.

My aim is to help you change your mindset so that you look at the opportunities around you rather than focusing on the threats. Of course, we can't ignore the threats – the things in life we have little control over, like rising bills and things that cause us financial harm – but rather than allowing these things to drag us down and make us enslaved by financial worry, I want to teach you how to use them as a motivator, a driving force to conquer your finances and make more money. The ability to make more money is a mindset; by changing the way you view the world and your personal circumstances, we can start to empower you to achieve your financial goals.

As I mentioned in Chapter 1, I am not trying to turn you into the next Jeff Bezos. People like Jeff, who have amassed unthinkable levels of money, have usually created something that the world wants – like Amazon. If I knew how to create the next big thing in tech or e-commerce, I'm afraid to say that I'd keep it to myself and hopefully be lying on a beach with my husband drinking cocktails without a care in the world. What I am trying to do is give you the tools and know-how to transform your finances in order to thrive rather than survive.

Look back at your bubble and let's see what you have: the assets you own that could earn you money, your skill set, your hobbies, and how they might be able to bring you financial gain.

I have an ethos which is to 'think small to earn big', which often confuses people because they see the word 'small' and decipher it as it's adjective, whereas I mean more your immediate environment. Think locally, in other words.

Rather than looking at the big, bad world and worrying how you could monetise opportunities within that vast space, look smaller, at the immediacy of what's around you and how you can utilise this for financial reward – look within your bubble. In doing so, you look at the world you know and understand best, which is a much less daunting place to inhabit and for us to start with.

Most people will have heard the term 'profit and loss' within business and as you go through *Money Maker*, you are going to start using and learning business terms to create your financial strategy for success.

'Profit and loss' merely means the financial statement of a company; it shows what revenue a business has made and what expenses it has incurred within a certain time period. So, when we apply this to your bubble, we need to look at your average monthly incomings and outgoings.

The challenge with this is we may often not have a clear understanding of or not want to admit the true picture of our outgoings over a financial year. What I mean is that we may not account for our annual holidays, spontaneous trips to the pub or impulse purchases. But in order for us to get an accurate and truthful oversight of your financial landscape, you will have to subscribe to my way of thinking. And whilst it may look like I'm over-inflating the picture, I assure you my method will put you in the best financial position that you ever have been.

Let's get started. What I want you to do, is to first list your everyday outgoings – bills, food, monthly subscriptions, direct debits etc. To this, add all the additional expenses you have over the year which may not fall within every calendar month:

> Holidays

> Seasonal celebrations – Christmas, Easter, religious holidays and events that require an additional outlay to normal months

> Birthdays and anniversaries

> Car insurance and tax

> Home insurance

> Weddings (is it just me or do we all feel like we have to re-mortgage to attend a wedding these days?)

Then, add in the incidentals which come out of nowhere, usually when finances are at their tightest:

> Dental work

> Fixing your car

> House repairs

> Vet bills

You can't possibly account for every incidental or additional expense, but by forecasting as much as possible you should be in a much better financial position to know how much you need to make in order to achieve all of your goals.

The other thing we can do to protect ourselves from any surprise expenses is to add in a safety net to create a monthly surplus which can cover unexpected outlays. I suggest aiming to put aside 15 per cent of your monthly incomings to create this.

On the next page I've started a handy profit and loss template you can adapt to list your income and expenses.

Profit and Loss Template

Name	
Net income	
Time period covered	

Income	
Wages	£
Tips	£
Other	£
	£
Total income	£

Expenses	
Rent/mortgage	£
Food	£

This will be your current P&L (profit and loss), but as we are aiming to thrive not just survive, I also want you to create an ambitious P&L on top of this.

Your ambitious P&L is going to be filled with your dream goals – so this might be an additional holiday a year, designer clothes and accessories, saving for a rainy day or even your dream car. You can choose to concentrate on one chapter to realise your money-making potential or follow the advice in multiple chapters to reach your goals sooner. Financial stability should be your first goal, but generating extra cash for those dream things you want in your life should also be achievable.

For example, if I were to create an ambitious P&L it would include things like:

> One extra family holiday a year = £150 per month

> One designer rucksack = £67 per month

> Savings = £100 per month

We can then add all of my ambitious goals up over the course of 12 months and see that I need to make an additional £3,804 a year to achieve this. The reason I suggest you create a monthly P&L target is so you can monitor if you are making the additional monthly income to reach your ambitious goals; if you fall short one month, you can use *Money Maker* to help you top up the following month's earnings. So, my monthly money-making target is £317.

If it's true that as a nation we are sitting on a £48 billion treasure trove of unwanted items, then maybe just one of my suggestions will earn you the entire amount of extra cash you need and my job here is done.

The final part of our great big life audit is to understand and be confident completing a tried and tested business technique that makes you analyse your strengths, weaknesses, opportunities and threats – SWOT. As you will see below, a SWOT analysis is made up of internal and external elements to help us assess these four aspects of your bubble. I did tell you that we'd be applying business terminology to your life, in order to achieve your goals!

	HELPFUL Will help you achieve your money-making objective	HARMFUL Will be harmful to you achieving your money-making objective
INTERNAL ORIGIN (your bubble)	Strengths	Weaknesses
EXTERNAL ORIGIN (your environment)	Opportunities	Threats

This can all sound rather serious but honestly its very simple and will help you focus on your bubble, what talents and treasures you have, whilst also understanding your weaknesses and the threats that could hinder your money-making potential.

As long as you are completely honest when conducting each SWOT analysis, you will save a lot of wasted time and effort. By identifying your weaknesses and threats, you will know the areas where you need to find solutions whilst also highlighting the positive skills you have and the amazing things you can do to make money. Remember, knowledge is power and power equals money.

Do a SWOT analysis for each money-making chapter as this will help you to identify which areas of this book will make you the most. Though I also suggest doing another once you've finished reading the whole book. That's because by then you will have a much greater understanding of your skills, areas that need improving, things you love to do and things you hate. With all the tips, tricks and skills I am about to teach you, you'll be able to understand where they sit within the SWOT in turn, enabling you to maximise your money-making potential.

To help you complete your first SWOT analysis, opposite is an example I have written based on my money-making plan to rent out items from my bubble to bring in additional cash (Chapter 6).

The first thing I always do before completing the SWOT is deciding the course of action. So I know I want to rent some things to make cash, but how much would I like to make and over what time period?

Dan Hatfield's Rental SWOT

The plan: to rent out my laptop, spare room and driveway. The financial goal: to make an additional £690 per calendar month on an ongoing basis.

Now I know what my goal is and what I am going to do to try and realise it, I can do some research. As I want to rent out things I own, I can go onto platforms where other people are doing the same to analyse the market and get a clear steer on what I could charge per month for my items.

Based on where I live and current market demand, I ascertain that I could rent out my:

> Laptop for £100 per month

> Spare room for £550 per month

> Driveway for £200 per month

Now I can move on and fill in my SWOT analysis, shown on the next page.

	HELPFUL to achieve the objective of making money
Internal origin (your bubble)	**My strengths:** 1. I am willing and able to designate two days a week to this money-making plan. 2. I am very tidy which should attract rental demand for the spare room. 3. I'm very good at networking and talking to people which will help me market and promote my rental items.
External origin (your environment)	**My opportunities:** 1. Our location – our property is in a desirable area, with lots of nice shops, restaurants and cafes a short stroll away, plus the Peak District is only a ten-minute drive away. 2. A new theatre is opening up which will likely drive up the demand for accommodation. 3. We are close to lots of business parks which often struggle to accommodate all parking needs. 4. As we work towards a more sustainable way of life, renting is fast becoming a preferred method for things like laptops, which we don't need access to 24/7/365.

	HARMFUL **to achieve the objective of making money**
Internal origin (your bubble)	**My weaknesses:** 1. I don't want to work weekends overseeing this. 2. My family often visit and need the parking space. 3. I'm disorganised and forgetful. 4. My husband currently uses the spare room as his office.
External origin (your environment)	**Threats:** 1. My laptop model will likely be superseded by a more modern version soon. 2. There is a new car park being built half a mile away. 3. A big industrial site is being renovated into bedsits and shared accommodation.

With this we have our SWOT analysis, I can use the findings to look at the areas of concern and whether or not I would be willing and able to overcome them. I'll go through my internal weaknesses and external threats to evaluate whether this is an achievable money-making endeavour.

Weaknesses:

1. *I don't want to work weekends overseeing this.* You can schedule your time so that management of these rental opportunities is taken care of on weekdays. You set the parameters of when you are renting your items, so make this clear in your advertising. There is still a big spare room rental market for people who just need weekday accommodation.

2. *My family often visit and need the parking space.* Most of the time, my family visit on the weekend when I don't want to be renting out my space, so this should be fine. If I do want to be able to offer it on weekends (because it doesn't require my management on the weekend) I can make sure I have a clear booking system so when arranging visitors who require parking, I can block out the dates when my family visit.

3. *I'm disorganised and forgetful.* I'll need to keep a diary and daily to-do list. I can schedule in time within my diary each day to keep on top of administration, make sure I have done the things needed to rent my items successfully and get someone to check in on my progress to keep me held accountable.

4. *My husband currently uses the spare room as his office.* This is a luxury and doesn't outweigh our need to supplement our income, so we can create an office space in the corner of our bedroom or the living room for the times he has to work from home.

Threats:

1. *My laptop model will likely be superseded by a more modern version soon.* Technology is growing exponentially and will continue to do so. I can keep an eye on the market to make sure I am charging the right amount, reducing this as newer models go on sale. There will still be people out there who don't need the most advanced laptop; they may just need to complete a course online or do some research, etc.

2. *There is a new car park being built half a mile away.* I will need to compete with their pricing. They are going to be charging £1 per hour and £20 per 24 hours, so I'll lower my pricing to be more competitive: 50p an hour and £10 per 24 hours. That's a tenner a day for doing nothing.

3. *A big industrial site is being renovated into bed sits and shared accommodation.* From my research, I know that supply is considerably lower than demand, so this is likely not to affect my rental potential. Also, if renting weekdays only, I am more flexible to businesspeople travelling for work, rather than those looking for long-term lets who might be more inclined to take contracts within the new development.

Evaluating my weaknesses and threats, I have found that there are solutions and methods I can deploy to overcome them. In conclusion, this could be an extremely lucrative money-making endeavour for me to reach my ambitious P&L goals.

When you have completed your P&L plus your ambitious P&L you will see what extra money you need to earn to achieve your goals. Then, after each chapter in *Money*

17

Maker, you can complete a SWOT analysis to understand what your strengths are, how to solve the issues with your weaknesses, grab the opportunities and counter-balance the threats.

That's all the boring business stuff out of the way. Now we can move forward, planning your next 12 months and the goals you want to achieve. Then I will teach you all my top tips and tricks to unlock the money-making potential within your bubble. Before you know it, you'll be a fully-fledged bubble entrepreneur and you'll be able to call yourself an official Money Maker.

THE CASH CALENDAR

Having completed your big life audit, we have a better understanding of your incomings and outgoings, and now you know how to complete a SWOT analysis you will be able to see what strengths, weaknesses, opportunities and threats are.

Now comes the fun part. I love a planner, somewhere where you can physically put your goals and aspirations, which is why I have drafted a simple 'Cash Calendar' template (see page 23), which you can use as inspiration to create your own to put up in your home so that you can track and achieve your money-making dreams.

Dan's Top Tip
Writing down your goals and putting them into a physical planner that you can see every day is a sure-fire way to keep you on track with your ambitions, making you far more likely to achieve them.

I want you to seriously consider what your goals are once you have completed reading *Money Maker*. What do you want to achieve financially over the next 12 months? Be ambitious but realistic. I want to enable you to have financial stability and teach you how you can use your bubble to make extra cash in order to achieve your personal dreams.

I find the easiest way to think about goals is to categorise them. This way you work out how much additional income you need to supplement your incomings and succeed.

Life landmarks

We often make the mistake of not planning for the things we take for granted, like friends and loved one's birthdays, anniversaries, date nights, weddings and births, etc. These landmarks seem small but can really impact your monthly P&L if you haven't planned for them in advance. By writing these on a calendar, you can manage your finances accordingly and identify if you need a money-making hack to cover any additional costs for a specific month.

Personal treats

What is the point of working so hard if we can't treat ourselves? My book is designed to help you manage your finances and teach you how to earn some extra cash so that you can reward yourself. So what are the luxuries that make you happy? Perhaps:

> A spa day

> Afternoon tea

> Dinner with friends

> Shopping for new clothes

> ❯ A cookery lesson

> ❯ Going to a concert

> ❯ The theatre

This list will totally depend on who you are and what you love to do, so these are just some suggestions. These treats should cost no more than roughly £100 – and remember, you are going to have to supplement your salary to achieve these, so it'll be unrealistic to put one of these in a calendar every day!

Big ticket purchases

This is the most ambitious part of your planning – those really big dream things that I want to help you turn into reality. These are going to take longer to achieve but if you follow all my money-making tips, there's no reason why you can't get there. Some big-ticket purchases might be:

> ❯ Dream holiday

> ❯ New kitchen

> ❯ Car

> ❯ Piece of fine jewellery

> ❯ Bike

> ❯ Designer outfit

Of course, I can't tell you what your dreams are, but I want you to start by putting one on a calendar for the first year. My ultimate hope is that you can add more as the years go on and you're succeeding as a bubble entrepreneur.

Savings

As we discussed in Chapter 2 – the Big Life Audit – I strongly advise putting aside at least 15 per cent of your earnings into a savings account. Not only does this provide you with a safety net to cover any unplanned incidentals (I once got stung with an awful dental bill) but it also starts to build up a nice little nest egg that can help you achieve your big-ticket purchases a lot sooner.

You might be in a more complex financial situation at present, so if 15 per cent is out of reach, tweak this to something that is achievable. As you take control of your finances, implementing my money-making tips, you can increase the amount you save over time.

Always remember to earn before you spend

All of my guidance will empower and guide you practically on ways to make additional money from your bubble. These are well researched, tried and tested methods but, as with all business ventures, there are no guarantees. You must truly understand your bubble to have a realistic idea of what cash a money-making hack could earn you. Then, completing a SWOT analysis after each money-making chapter will identify which of my tips will be best placed to help you achieve your dreams. It will also enable you to make a plan to handle any threats and weaknesses that may impact your money-making ability. Just remember that the economic environment and other global factors can hinder your efforts, even if you put the work in. So don't spend that cash until it's firmly in the bank.

Writing all your goals on a personal calendar will give you a clear oversight of what you need to earn in order to achieve them. As previously discussed, I want you to complete a monthly P&L to keep you on track and in control of your finances and your money-making.

In order to maximise your money-making potential, I suggest finding a combination of quick hustles and some longer-term methods you can use more regularly over the year. This will help provide a constant flow of additional cash, which will in turn make your financial dreams a reality sooner. Your cash calendar can be as simple as mine is below, where I write my monthly goals and what I could do in order to supplement my incomings to pay for the additional things I want.

PERSONAL CASH CALENDAR

Month	January
Goals	
Hustles	

THE ART OF THE BARTER

The art of bartering is one of the most important skills I am going to teach you to succeed with your money-making ambitions.

Bartering is as old as time; we humans bartered before the dawn of language and we naturally barter in everyday life. It happens all around us in various situations. In its purest form, to barter means to exchange goods or services without the use of money.

Throughout your entire life, you will be bartering when you might not even know it, whether it's within your career or family, with romantic partners or in another area of your life.

I have contemporised the term for the purpose of this book as it requires the same skills that you need to barter for non-monetary exchange, but I am here to teach you how to make money. So, for our purposes, 'the art of the barter' is the art of negotiating or haggling – it is using your skills of persuasion and clever use of language to get something for the best value possible.

Did you know that we could be missing out on £6.5 billion each year because we are 'too British to barter'? research conducted by the website Gumtree stated that our very British desire not to talk about money, not to try and negotiate or haggle, could cost each individual up to £500.[1] The research found that 46 per cent of respondents were too embarrassed to barter; 41 per cent were concerned it would make them seem rude and a staggering 80 per cent had never even attempted to barter their entire life. As someone whose entire livelihood is centred around securing the best deal, I am honestly shocked by these findings.

I have never come across a successful entrepreneur who hasn't mastered the art of the barter to secure the best possible price they can obtain an item for. You might also find it surprising that I advocate strongly for my clients to haggle with me. I get excited with the performative embrace as both sides go to battle to get the best deal. Remember, if a client barters with me to get my price down, they will walk away with the item they came for, at a price they have worked to get as low possible, leaving them empowered and satisfied.

I will often walk into high street shops and ask them for a better price, which is something I definitely learnt from my mum. She is a second-generation pawnbroker and she doesn't just barter at foreign markets; she will walk into a clothes shop in the UK and ask the sales assistant if they can reduce the price tag. If they can't, she will ask to speak with the manager and, with her expert skill, she will often secure anywhere from 10 to 40 per cent off the asking price. It was in these moments as a child that I first witnessed the excitement in her eyes and the adrenalin rush she was experiencing.

She didn't stop there, either; she brought bartering into the pawnbrokers and would negotiate the size and price of deals with clients using her clever techniques. If the client wanted a bigger discount, she would agree as long as they ordered more products, and herein the bartering battle commenced.

I can now relay this to you all as not only a skill for money saving but very much one for money making. By implementing it within my own business, I see multiple satisfied customers who are return clients because they are assured they are getting the best deal. On a micro level you might be thinking, 'But you lose a percentage of your profit!' Which is true, but on a macro level I build up a committed business relationship with repeat clients, who will not only deal with me in the future but also tell other businesses about the deals that can be struck in my shop.

This is why bartering is a mutually useful skill and, as a money-making bubble entrepreneur, I want you to embrace it and understand how this art form can benefit you. How it creates a less formal business relationship and, instead, a personal relationship founded on trust, respect and appreciation. Of course, the barter can also return to its earliest meaning and not have a monetary value. It could mean including things like free delivery or removal, free wrapping – some extras that help sweeten the deal and strengthen the relationship.

'So what is the best way to barter?' I hear you ask. Well, there isn't an exact science but there are lots of tips and tricks I have picked up and created over the years. Most of it comes from communication skills, a lot of it comes from confidence, and if you follow my advice you should be a bartering bubble entrepreneur in no time at all. First off, you need to:

1. Normalise bartering

There's a stereotyped assumption that in Britain we are extremely polite. But regardless of whether this is true or not, why do we think that bartering is being impolite? I'm not asking you to be rude or improper, far from it. All I want you to do is use a trait that our ancestors used in everyday undertakings from the start of civilisation. As I mentioned, bartering is merely negotiating, something you do when you're looking for better mobile phone deals, TV subscription packages or even insurance policies. In these situations, how often do you say, 'But this company have offered me the same for less'? Then a process of negotiation and discussion is undertaken where the company you are talking with tries to retain or secure your custom.

So, I want you to get comfortable with understanding how you can deploy the art of the barter into all of life's circumstances, especially when it comes to buying or selling goods to make money.

As discussed, this isn't rude. I want you to relax and never be confrontational or annoyed if someone offers you a price far lower than the price you'd like to achieve – they are merely exercising their right to barter to get the best deal. Take the emotion out of it; that isn't a personal attack they are playing their hand to secure as much of a discount as possible. So, keep your cool and have a few fun retorts up your sleeve. 'Do you want the shirt off my back, too?!' is one of my favourites.

2. Know the intrinsic value of an item or service.

Knowledge is power, as the old adage goes, and this is absolutely true. Too often, we don't do enough market research when it comes to deciding the price point for our goods or services. Without the knowledge of the appropriate market value, you have no idea of the parameters within which you can barter. When you accept that bartering is going to be a key factor in your negotiations, you accept the fact that you will need to have wiggle room in order to secure a sale. So, do your research.

Find out how much the item or service would cost the customer if they were buying it elsewhere, know and understand the variations of price points based on location or item's uniqueness, then set a price that you can successfully see a return within. People will always try and barter you down further, so be confident with the lowest you can go without it being a money loser. This has to include all costs to get this sale to market – whether that includes your time, marketing materials or anything else. If you have spent out to sell this item, you need to cover all of these costs and see a profit.

3. Understand the buyer

To successfully barter, you need to understand who you are bartering with. What is motivating this potential client? Are they in a hurry to make a purchase? Maybe they're absolutely in love with it and desperate to have it? Or perhaps they have been looking for an item like this for a long time.

Knowing their motivation will place your position for the start of the barter race. The keener they are, the stronger you can hold firm. But if they're sitting on the fence – maybe they are unsure of the colour of the item or whether they can afford it – then obviously you are going to need to do some stellar bartering to secure the sale.

Take into account these key factors when understanding the buyer:

Emotional factors

You need to understand and establish if the potential buyer has an emotional link to the item you are trying to sell. Is it something nostalgic that evokes memories of their childhood, maybe something that a loved one desperately wants or even something which will complete a set? When you understand whether the item has an emotional pull, then you are better informed about whether the monetary value has an impact on their decision or if you just need to engage with the emotion during barter to secure a deal.

Necessity factors

Does the buyer need the item or service you are selling? Maybe it's a costume for a specific fancy dress party, or they have to rent a high-end laptop to complete a work project. Whatever the reason, understanding how much they see the thing you are selling as a necessity will impact the art of the barter – needing things is a driving factor but not as strong as emotional, so you will need to barter harder to secure the sale.

Time factors

If what you are selling is needed urgently, you can secure a deal pretty quickly. But if your customer has time to shop around, you'll need to come in hard with the lowest price you can afford to secure a sale.

Financial factors

How often in life are we led by financial factors? I mean, why are you reading this book? Finance impacts so many of our decisions so this is a key area to understand when planning your barter. If finances are tough for your buyer, you'll need to barter with emotional or necessity factors. For example, explain how the item would look good on them or would improve their business venture, etc. Also, deploy other tactics like BOGOF (buy one get one free) or offer a larger discount if they buy two, and so on. Helping them to understand the deal they're getting with extras may encourage them to part with their cash and still have them leaving feeling rewarded.

All of these factors can be ascertained by asking some simple questions and analysing the answers. This will tell you what your bartering style needs to be:

> What attracted you to this item/service?

> Have you been searching for something like this for a long time?

> How quickly do you need this?

I'm not here to teach you to suck eggs, so I'm sure I don't need to list all the potential questions you can ask, but you are ultimately trying to understand their motivation, which will inform you how strongly or passively they want what you are selling. Once you understand this, you'll know what barter technique to deploy in order to succeed.

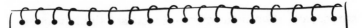

Dan's Top Tip

I often see salespeople make the cardinal sin of sales – talking at people. Don't do this. Ask questions and pay attention to the answers. Your potential clients' answers will guide you to the right approach.

4. Keep it friendly and respectful

A passive barterer is likely to be walked all over, whereas an aggressive barterer is more likely to lose the deal completely. I've seen far too many businesses and private sellers be led by emotion and thus either gone on the offensive or started so forcefully that it has terrified a potential client and made them walk away. Neither of these approaches are going to secure you sales. It has been proven psychologically that we are more inclined to buy from those we like; therefore, we need to take a friendly and respectful approach with our bartering technique, and it doesn't hurt to add a smile and some gentle humour.

Here are a few things to remember when you are interacting with potential clients:

Re-read any written communication with a potential buyer

How often have you heard a friend assume a tone from a text message or a colleague get angry with an email? The digital age is a wonderful thing but we are emotional by nature and often assume a tone that suits our feelings at the time. Or perhaps it's an exclamation point which you have read as anger and strong feelings when in reality it was simply meant to show something is light-hearted. So re-read before you send and check your use of words and punctuation can't be interpreted the wrong way.

Evoke the feeling you want your client to have (even if over the phone)

I cannot tell you how many times I have felt my husband's eyes roll when we are on the phone. Maybe it's a sixth sense, (who knows?), but I know I get a sense from a person's tone of voice, even over the phone. Always project a positive attitude – be happy and helpful and remember to smile.

Listen to your customer or client

I never shut someone down if they are bartering for a better deal. I listen to their justification and think quickly on my feet to either retort or concede. Remember: you know your price point, so you know where you can go to if you need to.

Find common ground

A vital part of bartering is to understand and show acceptance of the person you are bartering with. You need to build a rapport with them to achieve a positive outcome for you both. Share past experiences with them, the history or your item or story of your service; use emotive factors to help them understand that they want what you have to offer. I'll say it one last time (though I actually can't promise it's the last time): we buy off people we like! And that does deserve an exclamation mark.

5. Use nonverbal cues

Nonverbal cues are a brilliant way to show respect, interest and agreement, and to share a reaction. Remember: we want to be engaging, so a smile helps express happiness, joy and kindness. It is vital that we make eye contact to confirm interest in a conversation. Even mirroring a person's body language is proven to subconsciously indicate interest.

6. Understand how offers and discounts can help

Providing incentives means that everyone wins. When bartering, if you feel like you are losing the deal, think about what you can do to secure it instead. It could be to offer a BOGOF deal, or better discounts the more you buy, even bundles. Help buyers to understand that they are getting a great deal because you have offered something extra as part of your bartering negotiation. Verbalise how you are willing to lose the profit from a t-shirt to include it with the sale of a coat the buyer is already interested in. Or if offering services, add a sixth for free when they buy five. It's human nature to want more for less, so work out in advance what additions you can offer without compromising your profit, so that when you are bartering, you have a clear trajectory of where you can take the conversation to secure the deal.

Now that you have learnt the key foundations to bartering, you need to put them into practice – I cannot emphasise enough how important it is to practise. At first, especially if you are nervous, why not practise your bartering technique with friends or family? When you are confident you can take yourself to a flower market or car boot sale to further develop your technique. But practice really does make perfect with this skill set. As we discussed, confidence is key, so in order for people to trust what you are saying, you need to believe in your ability to tell them.

Success rarely comes from merely taking advantage of our strengths but, instead, from the ability to identify and understand our weaknesses and how we can improve upon them. It might be that, whilst bartering, you offer a big discount too quickly out of nervousness, or that you are too greedy with your profit line and deter people too soon with a hard approach.

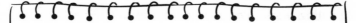

Dan's Top Tip

You can achieve great profits with a high turnover of items for a smaller profit margin per item. A higher profit margin usually requires a longer sales strategy and more of your time. As long as you are making a profit, make sales regularly and quickly.

You have to practise the notion of difficult customers. I'm afraid to say that they are everywhere; not everyone will have read my book and understand the etiquette of respectful bartering, so be prepared for the often-difficult buyer who doesn't have the time or patience to be nice. You can win them over with your bartering technique, though. It's all about style and approach.

Remember that even a difficult customer wants the desired outcome – they ultimately want something you have for the lowest possible price. If their bartering technique is harsh and abrasive, respond with calm and be amenable nonetheless.

Try these simple exercises to strengthen your ability to deal with difficult customers. Get a friend or family member to act in the following manners:

> They keep interrupting you whilst you talk.

> They are aggressive in their approach.

> They ask for unrealistic discounts.

> They think there is a problem with the item/service they want to buy.

> They think the quality of what you are selling is questionable.

By roleplaying these different scenarios, you will learn how to react to them. Remember, you are only ever to react with friendliness and respect. So, practise not getting aggravated and not allowing yourself to lose your cool, and definitely learn to appreciate that you can never know what someone else is going through. You can always sacrifice a sale if you decide dealing with this person isn't worth it. You can say the conversation isn't working or you are clearly on different pages, but stay calm and in control regardless of the buyer who approaches you.

There are so many sales scenarios that you will face so taking the time to learn the art of the barter and practising what works for you will benefit you in the long run and secure you greater sales, greater profit and greater satisfaction.

When you're the buyer

The art of the barter isn't just for selling, though. In later chapters, we are going to learn how to make money from buying items and selling them on, so this key skill will be crucial in all your money-making adventures.

Remember, when selling an item or service, you start the bartering process as you have set the price. When buying, you have to understand the market to know a realistic price to try and engage a seller with that won't make them think you are a chancer, meaning they disengage from the barter race from the outset. So, confidence is yet again key on the opposite side of the barter race. When purchasing, you need to trust that you can secure the purchase for the price you want to pay.

Similar rules apply when buying:

1. **Keep it nice:** As with selling, you should always maintain a pleasant and calm approach when bartering, but don't be afraid to be firm. Nonverbal cues are as important for a seller as they are for a buyer. Start with a smile, use a non-offensive statement like 'What's your best price for this?', as it will break the ice and start a conversation or the bartering process with much more ease.

2. **Know your limit and the market:** When selling, you need to know the base value of the product or service you are offering and this is the same for buying. Know the value of what you want to purchase and how far you are willing to go to secure it.

36

3. **Understand the sellers:** This is quite literally the flip barter technique of when selling. Ask questions like: 'How long have you been trying to shift this?' 'How quickly do you want this gone?' Again, it's about asking questions to help you understand your barter partner's motivation. Just in this situation, you want to know the motivation of why they want to sell. The quicker someone wants to be rid of something, the better the opportunity you have to barter your way to a great deal.

4. **Whereas with sales you offer multi-buys, when buying ask for them:** In reality, most sellers want rid of their goods and, as I said in my earlier top tip, a frequent but regular profit is better than no profit at all. So, ask for multi-buys or offer to pay less per item for more of them. This creates bartering harmony – both lanes of the barter race compete and win.

5. **Cash is still king:** Whatever is going on in the world, cash remains king and so having the right amount of cash in your pocket – or at least the right amount you are willing to part with – can secure you a sale quicker. There are often fees payable on bank transfer and credit card payments, which means that a seller will always appreciate a cash sale to maximise profit.

Whether buying or selling, always watch your language. I know we discussed keeping it friendly and respectful, but we must also pay special attention to the words that we use. Certain phrases or words can obstruct a sale or purchase instantly. When bartering, we must always convey confidence and conviction. An indication of uncertainty or wavering will automatically put you in a weaker position to barter, so banish these un-barter friendly phrases:

> I think

> Could I

> Maybe

> Perhaps

> Possibly

> May I

> I might.

And any other passive words and phrases. Instead, approach bartering with a kind yet assertive manner, by using words and phrases like:

> I want

> I'm willing to pay

> The price I know to be fair is

> Let's shake on this price.

It seems like simple advice but trust me, using the wrong word or phrase when negotiating with a seasoned barterer will do you no favours.

The 7-38-55 rule

Finally, pay specific attention to the 7–38–55 rule. Professor Albert Mehrabian from the University of Central Los Angeles created this rule. The fundamentals of which are this:

When speaking,

> 7 per cent of the message is conveyed through the words used

> 38 per cent of the message is conveyed by the tone of the speaker's voice

> 55 per cent of the message is conveyed by their body language and face.

In layman's terms, we focus very little on the words people say, and instead learn more from their mannerisms and characteristics. This is why the art of the barter is all about knowledge, confidence, approachability and likeability.

Be the person that people want to interact with, have a laugh and a joke, engage with their interests and hobbies, but, most importantly, have fun with the art of the barter. If you can perfect this gift of the gab, you'll be able to handle any situation with confidence and persuade people to see your perspective, to either buy your goods or to sell theirs to you at a decent price.

JACKPOT IN YOUR HIDDEN TREASURES

Our homes can be an absolute treasure trove when it comes to unwanted items that have the potential to make you money. It is generally considered that, on average, we each have 42 unused items that could be worth up to £3,000. That's just for unused items – I'm pretty confident I could raise that figure and make you even more money if we looked around our homes for things we could live without and those items we rarely use. On top of this, a staggering 70 million homeware items valued at £2.2 billion are thrown into landfill each year.

I want to enable you to be able to spot the hidden treasures in your home and turn them into cash. Not only will I show you what items you might have that can sell on for a decent profit but, more importantly, where you should sell them to maximise your money-making potential. One thing I have learnt in my career of selling and buying is that the point-of-sale location can increase your profitability tenfold.

The first thing we are going to have to do to release the

money-making potential from our unused goods is to put our homes through a sieve – by which I mean have a decent clear out. Research in the USA claims that Americans have, on average, 300,000 items in their homes. Whilst this figure will fluctuate country to country, I'm confident that those in the developed world will roughly be the same. I know for certain that I do not use or benefit from 300,000 items on a day-to-day basis. Therefore, we need to isolate what is of value, and how and where we can sell it.

Going through our home and evaluating what items we use and don't and what we would be prepared to sell on is a strangely liberating exercise, not to mention a profitable one. I'm here to show you how to spot things that could be worth money, but for items that don't hold a value, we should clear them out regardless because a clear home will help you achieve a clear mind. Every 18 months, if I haven't used something I sell it. I wait 18 months due to the seasonality of some items, but I have friends who are much stricter who have monthly clear outs to make additional money.

I have five very easy to follow rules, to put your own home through a sieve:

1. Be tough, don't let emotions rule your decisions

As a seasoned pawnbroker, I regularly meet with people who have items that were passed down to them from family members or that they purchased and have an emotional connection to. These will undoubtedly have an emotive pull, but if you need to make more money, you must be ruthless. Here's a technique to help you to visualise how such items could benefit you even more . . .

Pick an item you feel an emotional connection with. I find family jewellery often works well. Then tap into your memories to remind yourself what it means to you whilst also thinking about its monetary value. Then physically write down how that money could come in handy – maybe it could clear some bills, go towards a trip or help purchase something you need.

What you're doing here is separating the emotion from the logic in order to best decide how this item will benefit your financial needs. Memories stay with us for our lifetime, so don't allow a physical item to make you disbelieve you'll lose that memory if you part with it.

2. Be methodical

It's all too easy at home to take on a more relaxed approach – I find I take a less urgent stance on things I need to do, whereas in my shop, I have to-do lists and I'm extremely focused. So, I want you to put systems in place and treat this process with the professionalism of running a business. Remember, you're a bubble entrepreneur. If you are thorough and methodical, you will be able to make much more money.

My top tip here is to operate room by room and do not move on to a new location until you have finished completely. Empty the cupboards and drawers, and get anything tucked on top of the wardrobe or behind the sofa out in front of you. Then do an inventory using my handy template below:

Item	Price	Price achieved	Date sold

Just like the emotional advice above, writing things down improves your chances of retaining the information, so it is a great method to track all your business endeavours and keep an eye on how much money this activity is earning you.

3. Don't dwell on prices

All you need to do at this point is to establish if something has a sellable value. We will fine tune the pricing strategy later; all we need to understand right now is that there is a ballpark figure we are confident it can make.

4. One person's junk is another's treasure

We've all had the clothes from an aunty for Christmas or the birthday gift that was totally off the mark, which we throw to the back of a cupboard and forget about. Remember, just because something isn't your style, or doesn't have a use in your home, it doesn't negate how valuable or attractive it could be to someone else.

5. Understand the difference between pre-loved, vintage and antique

Some might use the term pre-loved to categorise anything that has been used or owned by someone else, but I find it useful to date stamp pre-loved, vintage and antique to help us understand an item's value and the best place to sell it. So, for this purpose, think of pre-loved as anything up to 20 years old, vintage is items made over 20 but under 100 years ago and antique is anything made over 100 years ago.

Once you have put your home through a sieve, we can start to look at the prices you can get. Obviously, I am not going to value and price up 300,000 items . . . so you're going to have to do a bit more work to research and check what similar items are selling for. Instead, let's go through some of the most common rooms in a home to look at some examples of money-making treasures.

The kitchen

Of all the rooms in your home, you won't find more unused gadgets than in the kitchen.

According to a recent study (by Tap Warehouse), British households could make, on average, £822 from selling unused kitchen gadgets.[2] On top of this, research (from Recycle Your Electricals) also found that households in the UK own 18.2 million kitchen electricals that are rarely or never used, such as popcorn makers, chocolate fountains and bread makers.[3] The average amount you can expect to raise from these items is £27 but there are also some big hitters like kitchen aides that can make you, on average, £190.

The unused gadgets that can command a decent price include:

> Ice cream makers

> Sous Vide machine

> Pasta makers

> Waffle maker

> Bread makers

> Juicers

> Blenders

> Slow cookers

> Air fryers

> Chef's knives

> Chocolate fountains

> Electric stand mixers

> Toastie makers

> Coffee machines

> Fondue sets

Items of less value but still worth money, include:

> Soufflé dishes

> Cake tins

> Tupperware

> Pots and pans

> Woks

> Knife sharpeners

> Spiralisers

> Bamboo steamers

> Tagines

> Salt and pepper shakers

Vintage and antique kitchen items are also massively popular. In my experience, these items garner a greater international interest:

> Ice cream makers

> Weighing scales

> Pots and pans

> Jars and storage tins

> Jelly moulds

Don't forget to check the value of your vintage cookery books too, as many of these are extremely collectable.

My favourite vintage kitchenware item to look out for is Pyrex. The most valuable pieces come from the 1950s up to the 1980s, with the value dependant on the colour and pattern. I found one that sold for over £4,700 and if that isn't enough to motivate you, I'm not sure what would be.

Some of the most valuable Pyrex dishes are:

> Lucky in Love 1959 is known as the holy grail of Pyrex. Much sought after, it could earn you £3,000.

> Promo Gourmet Gold casserole 1961. One sold in an online auction for £1,500.

> Avocado Spring Blossom Crazy Daisy casserole hails from the 1970s and one sold for £1,250.

> Turquoise Snowflake round cake pan is one of the most collected patterns – they can sell for roughly £1,000.

> Pink Stems oval casserole server is very retro cool and selling for around £550.

Even the most common vintage pieces can still retail for £50 to £100.

Dining room/area

According to RightMove, mentions of dining rooms in house sales listings has fallen by 28 per cent.[4] This room, which was once a status symbol, proving you were wealthy enough to have a room just for eating in, can now often be found empty. As we change the way we live or the need for extra space in our homes evolves, a lot of people are converting dining rooms in to home offices, cinema rooms, a playroom or another bedroom (check out Chapter 6 to unlock how to monetise this room).

With fewer of us using a dining room for its traditional purpose, you could sell all the furniture within it. Or, if, like me, you still enjoy a family meal around the table a couple of times a week, you can still find treasure you can turn into a little jackpot:

> Dining table and chairs are often expensive so buying pre-loved is popular.

> Vintage tablecloths – cross reference any vintage tablecloths you have on Etsy as there is a market with international buyers for some specific types.

> Dressers are popular for various rooms around the home nowadays.

> Silver and silver-plated cutlery is very collectable. You might even be able to sell stainless steel sets. Whether a full set, incomplete or even odd collections, they generally hold their worth. A full canteen of cutlery will sell quickest and for the most money. Whilst most eras sell, mid-century is very desirable.

> China should never be thrown away without checking because the most unexpected designs and collections can be worth decent money.

> Crystal – good quality drinking vessels always go for great money.

> Silver candlesticks fly off the second-hand shelf but other materials can also sell well.

> Photo frames, whether silver or other material, are decent earners.

The living room

This is generally the most cluttered room of a home, so you have the opportunity to really clean up here – and I mean that financially as well as aesthetically.

> Sofas

> Coffee tables

> Mirrors

> Bookcases

> Rugs

> Ornaments

All of these items will sell well for you and most living rooms will also be full of technology like computer consoles and DVD players that can make you money. Find out more about this in Chapter 7, where I show you how to make cash from your tech. In addition to tech, the items you put in them can make you money:

> DVDs and even VHS tapes can make you a mint. As we've previously discussed, nostalgia plays a massive part in consumerism, so we are currently seeing huge demand for items from the 1980s and 1990s. One original VHS tape of *Back to the Future* recently found itself in the middle of a bidding war, with the final price an astonishing £8,000. Do your research but anything unique with a misprint or mistake can attract higher valuations, and the classics like Disney usually sell for a decent amount.

> Books. As a nation we throw away around 150 million books a year and although we continue our way through the digital revolution, there are loads of people like me, who can't beat the enjoyment of reading a physical book. Always check if you have any limited edition books. The hardback, limited edition Harry Potter set is worth a fortune, but if in a decent condition, most books you'll be able to sell on Amazon marketplace.

Dan's Fun Fact:

In 2022, 19 per cent more tapes had been sold than in the previous year and overall, there has been a 94.7 per cent increase in cassette tapes popularity since 2020.

> CDs, cassette tapes and vinyl can earn you plenty of cash, especially if you have lots of it you are willing to sell in bulk.

Old cassette tapes typically sell for £1 to £3.50, but there are some big value, limited editions out there. For example:

> Linkin Park was originally called Xero and a cassette from 1997 in this name has sold for £3,720.

> A specialist release of Pink Floyd's *High Fidelity* could make you £800.

> A Depeche Mode 1980 demo tape once sold for nearly £1,400.

Old CDs sell for between £1 and £2, but, like cassettes, some of the rarer ones can be worth a fortune. For example:

> There are only ten *Star Wars: Episode II – Attack of the Clones* original motion picture soundtracks in existence, driving its value up to £11,000.

> A *U2: Special Collection 1980–1987* sealed CD sold for £6,898.

Vinyl is currently enjoying a 30-year high in popularity and even mass-produced copies of certain records can sell for around £12. Rare editions can get you to the thousands:

> An original *David Bowie* by David Bowie 1969 Australian pressing sold for £7100.

> The very first copy of Kate Bush's *The Sensual World* (a limited edition for Unicef) sold for £2,200 at auction.

The rarity of your CDs, cassettes and records, plus the artist's popularity and the condition of the item will always affect the price you can charge, but even if you have the mass-produced copy, they sell well. Try doing bundles to clear them quicker.

Bedrooms

Unlike the living room, we generally don't clutter our bedrooms (teenagers exempt) because this is our sanctuary and place of rest, but that doesn't mean we don't have money to be made from them.

As will be discussed in Chapter 7, TVs can not only make you lots of money but there are various wellbeing reasons why you shouldn't have one in your sleeping quarters. Other things you can sell, especially if you are making over your bedroom are:

> Bedside tables

> Lamps

> Headboards

> Dressing tables

> Chairs

> Curtains and blinds

> Rugs

> Wardrobes

Children's bedrooms

According to recent research, it costs between £150,000 to £200,000 to raise a child in the UK, so we therefore have a lot of stuff relating to our kids. When no longer needed, that could be making you a lot of money. If your child has grown up and left home then it's time to clear out and turn a profit, but if your child is still at home then, age dependant, consult with them or involve them in the selling process, offering a reward for helping you to make some money and decluttering the home.

> Parents spend an average £736 a year on children's clothing. Research indicates that 7 in 10 parents hold on to clothes that they could sell. You could be earning about 20 per cent of the original price if the clothes are in good condition.

> Research suggests that children have at least four toys that they have never played with. Furthermore, they get bored of a toy after around 36 days on average. To top this off, 1 in 3 parents admit to throwing away perfectly good toys, which equates to 162 million believed to be put into landfills each year that could have been resold.

> It is estimated that we spend £6,000 on our first newborn. Further estimates state that £1.6 billion of these items that could have been sold on end up in landfill.

> Car seats can sell for 30–50 per cent of their original retail price. You have to be sure they are in perfect condition as safety always beats profitability. Each platform will have specific safety requirements to sell

this item so ensure you adhere to their regulations.

> Prams cost us, on average, £340 and yet 38 per cent of parents admit to never selling theirs on. You can sell them second-hand for roughly 40 per cent of their RRP.

> We spend a similar amount on cots which can also yield a 40 per cent of the original price if in good condition.

The garage

In the UK, we have 11.4 million garages, yet it's reported that we only use half of them to park car in and the others are being used for storage. That could mean there are 5.7 million garages filled to the rafters with items that we could sell on.

This is just a brief overview of the jackpots you might have in the various rooms around your home. Don't forget, our homes contain so much, so every now and again, do a thorough walk around and look through to challenge yourself to see if you use and in fact need certain items. If you have an attic, storage unit or shed, now is the time to clear these out and see if you could be sitting on some hidden treasures. Latest research suggests that the garden shed could be holding up to £2,600 worth of unwanted items that could earn you a shedload of cash.

Dan's Top Tip

Whenever you put your home through a sieve, remember to keep an eye out for rare items that can be worth a fortune. The subsequent chapters discuss how to monetise these items by renting, finding collectables, high-value tech and clothes.

Gold

One rare item most of you will have in your home is gold. It is estimated that each of us may have £1,700 worth. But before you rush to find and sell it, I would advise you find and store it.

On average, the price of gold has risen 11 per cent per year. If you look at that next to the rate of inflation which, is around 2.82 per cent per year (from 1989 to 2023), it's clear that gold yields a fantastic return. There are five different carats of gold recognised in the UK:

> 9ct – this has 37.5 per cent purity and is the most common gold found in the UK.

> 14ct – this has 58.5 per cent purity and is usually imported from countries such as USA and some European countries.

> 18ct – this is 75 per cent pure gold and is used in more expensive jewellery, especially wedding

and engagement rings or to hold fine stones like diamonds.

> 22ct – this is 91.6 per cent pure gold but, due to the rising costs, its popularity lowered in the 1960s and today is quite rare.

> 24ct – this is 99.9 per cent pure gold and is mainly held as investment coins and bars.

I am fascinated by gold and it's one of the main items that comes through my business. But if you can afford to keep it, it could be much more valuable for you to sell in later life or retirement, due to the fact that it's value generally remains stable and doesn't decline over time.

Sports and hobbies

Back to items that you should sell. Ones you can find in any room around your home are those we use for our hobbies, but did you know that a recent study found that most adults drop a hobby after only 16 months? There will be various life factors that give good reasons for this, but it means that we could have a treasure trove of desirable hobby items collecting dust around the home. For example:

> Golf clubs and clothing

> Tennis racquets

> Football shirts

> Rugby shirts

> Roller blades and skates

> Fishing equipment

> Photographic equipment

> Painting equipment

> Musical instruments, such as guitars, violins, pianos, trumpets

> Sewing machines (my husband has one of these that he swears he's going to start making us shirts with . . . Five years later and I'm still shopping for shirts).

You'll notice that sporting items appear quite regularly with hobbies, and that's because us Brits have an estimated £1.5 billion of unused gym and sports equipment. That's about £200 worth of cash per household not being fully realised.

Some of the bigger items of sports equipment, such as running machines, exercise bikes and weight sets, often get stored in rooms we don't use very often, so they go unnoticed. Dig these out and research the prices so that you can transform them into cash quickly by selling them on Facebook Marketplace – or, for less leg work, try webuygymequipment.com.

Another sporting item that can make you a nice little profit is bikes. Research from the Bike Club shows that roughly 34 per cent of the adult population have one or more unused bikes and 15 per cent have one or more unused child's bike. Dependant on condition, make and model, the average adult bike can sell for a decent £100 and some children's bikes can secure £80 to £130. Gumtree and Facebook Marketplace are great for selling unwanted bikes.

Tools

We spend £20 billion on tools a year and research suggests that at least £2 billion of these are unused and 10 per cent haven't even been opened. Power tools and even hand-held tools are a massive market, so a thorough clear-out can make you a lot of money quickly.

There are loads of places you can sell tools, including cash4tools.co.uk and thetoolsquirell.co.uk, or your usual eCommerce sites.

Old magazines, newspapers and their supplements

After the death of Her Majesty Queen Elizabeth II, news-papers depicting this historical event were being listed and sometimes selling for hundreds of pounds. Big headlines can often mean big money, so I recommend buying papers and magazines that highlight monumental events, such as significant births, deaths and historical occasions. I find it's best to sell them immediately as they can demand a higher price. For instance, newspapers covering the Queen's passing were being listed, and in some cases selling, for £200 in the days just after her death, whereas nowadays, they will likely sell for £5, which is still a profit, but the quicker you act the more you can make.

Then there is always the exception to the rule. If you have any papers with the specific headlines below, they can earn you impressive cash:

> The Cuban missile crisis £500

> The death of Elvis Presley £300

> The Great Train Robbery £200

> Prince Charles and Lady Diana's wedding £200

> Death of Diana, Princess of Wales £100

Home collectibles

Whilst I've already talked about some of the furniture you may have in the different rooms of your house, it is worth quickly looking at some of the most sought-after items from the 1950s to 1990s, which are having a particular resurgence:

> 1960s and 1970s TV side boards. Some Scandinavian and British oak ones have been reaching over £1,000, but for a mass-produced version, £450 is a reasonable valuation.

> 1970s and 80s leather recliners are selling online for £400–£500 and even if when a little tired, they can hold onto their value.

> Desks. As an increasing number of people are working from home, demand for vintage desks has surged. Especially old school desks, military desks and others with a quirky history to them. Mid-century desks can sell for anything from £100 to £1,000.

Cash from trash

Not all of the treasures in your home will land you the big jackpot, but there is still cash to be had from your trash. Items that are broken, faulty or things that you would generally discard as useless, all have a market and potential to make you some money. You may be surprised of some of the items people will buy from you:

Broken household goods

We are a country which is guilty of putting 2 million tonnes of electrical goods in landfill, but these items can actually make you money whilst also helping the environment. Broken and defunct electricals are still in high demand because there are likely still parts of that electrical item which can be salvaged and used. Whether a TV, hair straighteners or a computer which won't turn on, Zarax.co.uk and techhair.co.uk are two of the companies that will buy them from you. There are loads of other sites where you can sell your broken and unwanted electricals, so do your research. It won't make you your jackpot but we're still talking hard cash.

Broken furniture

There is a massive social trend of upcycling, which is not only sustainable but also means you have a market to sell your broken old furniture for it to be repurposed and reused.

Real trash

The core of toilet and kitchen rolls, coat hangers and empty perfume bottles can bring the sweet smell of cash. Generally, you need to sell them in bulk, but items I often put into recycling really are selling:

> Egg cartons can sell for various amount but you can expect people to pay £10 for 20.

> Toilet and kitchen roll cores can sell for 7p–8p each.

> Used Yankee candle jars have a market value of £9 for four.

> Empty perfume and aftershave bottles seem to be a real money-maker. Run-of-the-mill style bottles can fetch you £1 but some higher-end ones can fetch you £4 and luxury designer or bespoke designs sell for £20 to £40.

> Old instruction manuals are similar to books; some people prefer the hard copy to use rather than searching the internet. I have loads of these unopened and they can retail between £4 and £20.

> I recently saw a collection of 100 wine corks sell for £200. On average, this quantity of corks sells for £50 to £100, whereas champagne corks can sell for more.

I could spend hours talking about all the random, quirky and interesting home items people will buy, but the key principle is to research what you have and have a look whether there is demand for it. I think you'll be surprised what trash you can turn into cash.

Even if you don't have all the items we have discussed, a piece of research from eBay suggests that most homes could make at least £1,252 with a quick home declutter:

> Bikes £284

> Tablet £171

> Video game console £158

> Smart watch £124

> Ping pong table £120

> Vacuum cleaner £86

> Hair dryer £70

> Car seat £65

> Pod and capsule coffee machine £60

> Air bed £40

> Christmas tree £38

> Juicer £36

These prices will fluctuate depending on condition, age, inflation – and I'm not so sure how many of us have a ping pong tables to flog – but it is interesting to see what unused items we have lying around the house which could secure us a jackpot payday.

Researching prices before you put anything up for sale is vital. We know that too high and we'll price ourselves out of the market and too low can make some buyers think it's too good to be true. So we need to turn detective, look at multiple selling platforms and work out the sweet spot for what we have. Once we've evaluated supply and demand, we have a much clearer pricing strategy.

Below are just a few of the methods I use to value my second-hand items:

The Google app

This has become many trader's secret weapon and I am sure there are plenty of people out there who won't be happy that I've told you about it but I am here to make you money.

To operate it, you just open the app and head to the search bar up the top, then click on the camera icon to take a picture of what you have. The app will recognise your item and bring up objects similar to what you have. Scroll along to the shopping section and you'll find prices that your item is currently selling for. The app doesn't always match exactly so sometimes you may need to add in further information to get realistic prices.

The eBay app

This works in a similar way to the Google app above but once you've opened the app, clicked the search bar and then the camera symbol – you'll then be directed to the barcode symbol. You can point your camera at the barcode of your item and the app will scan this and list identical products for sale. I always click on the 'sold items' section to see what price items have actually gone for. You can use this app without the barcode function just by using pictures.

Skim the market

Well, that's what I call this process anyway. Don't just look to one site to determine your pricing. This book is full of selling sites, so go through as many as possible to understand your best price. Cross-reference condition, age and rarity to best price match and find yourself becoming an in-demand seller.

Get friendly with the natives

Again, my phrase, not an official term, but there are so many enthusiasts, online forums, groups and fan clubs that you can join to better understand the value of your items. Talk to people who actively buy and collect these items to learn more about how much they are willing to pay for some of the things you may have.

These are all great ways to learn what you could sell your general second-hand items for, but if you have stumbled across something you think could be that jackpot treasure then I suggest doing some more detailed work to make sure you're going to earn what your item is worth. Whether a rare toy, limited edition item or inherited jewellery, these items will need specialist advice. To do this, you could always get an insurance valuation. Remember, though, that an insurance valuation is always higher than your retail price because it's the price it would cost to source and replace an item but it is a good place to start.

Pawnbrokers like me have a broad range of knowledge so can pretty much give you a valuation for most items. You don't need a big, fancy and expensive valuer; I suggest spending no more than £30 to get yourself a valuation. Whatever reputable person you get to value your item should be able to tell you the recommended retail price for it and might even offer you a price to buy it themselves. This is great research and insight, but don't accept the first offer – go away and cross-reference this pricing with other places to make sure you're making the most money.

Auction houses are also a great way to get valuations. Many, up and down the country, have open days where you can get free advice on the value of your items. They do this in the hope that you will agree to sell your item with them, but you are under no obligation to do so and I would always advise you to get a few more prices before you commit to the sales room. When considering an auction house make sure you understand the additional fees associated with this sales route.

Lastly, remind yourself of the original retail cost of your items brand new. You can use this within your sales strategy – highlight the RRP and then give your second-hand price to reinforce the bargain you are offering to the customer.

When you have a rough idea of your pricing, you need to do a final check for anything that may affect this. Imperfections, missing parts, wear and tear can all impact how much you can charge, so once you have looked at the market, re-examine the condition of your item next to the price of ones you've seen sold; if yours is in better or worse condition, adjust your prices appropriately.

Wherever you are going to sell your hidden treasures, be prepared to negotiate. The second-hand market is a lively and fascinating arena, but it is well populated, so you need to be able to stand out from the crowd and give people a reason to buy with you. You've already done all the research I have suggested, so place yourself slightly cheaper than your biggest competition and also be willing to accept a little less. I've taught you how to barter, but everyone you are selling to will also be well versed in this art form, and they are out for a bargain.

Finally, don't forget to include any fees you might have to pay when pricing up your goods. A lot of online sites or physical locations may have a set cost or commission percentage associated with any sale, so you need to factor this into your pricing strategy to make sure you're making a profit.

As I mentioned at the beginning of this chapter, where

to sell your item is important as it can really impact your money-making potential. Throughout *Money Maker*, I will give you recommendations for certain categories, but the number of places you can sell is pretty limitless, which is why I always harp on about doing the research for your specific needs. In a very generalised way, there are two ways you can sell:

Selling direct to buyers

This is the way you are likely to make the most money, but you will have to work for it. Once you have set your price and understood any charges associated with where you are selling, apart from a little bartering you will be pretty clear on what your items will earn you. The downside to selling it yourself is that it is much more time consuming, as you have to undertake all parts of the selling process, from taking pictures to writing descriptions, answering questions and eventually posting it out. You also must deal with the aftercare and if your customer has any issues then you are responsible.

Selling to dealers or resellers

Selling to either a dealer or a reseller is the quickest way for you to release cash from your unwanted goods. The hassle is taken away in this version of selling, as once a dealer or reseller has agreed a price with you, you take your money and have no further responsibilities. This does lower your money-making potential because a dealer or reseller is taking on the job of sourcing a buyer and processing a sale, so they will offer you a lower price than you can garner from doing it yourself to ensure that they can make a profit for their time and effort.

Both options have an appeal. You might be time poor and therefor a dealer/reseller site can earn you cash very quickly but for a lower premium. Or, if you have the time to undertake every aspect of selling it yourself, you will earn more money in the long run.

However, you cannot have it both ways. You cannot expect to make the top price by using a reseller or dealer. I often have people come into my shop wanting to sell me a watch, but they want a price they have seen on an ecommerce site like eBay. These two worlds are separate: a person on eBay is doing the work and aftercare themselves so they can demand a higher price; I am a dealer and have shop costs and staff to cover, so will have to offer you less for taking on the task of securing a sale, but you will have the cash quicker.

If you are excited about selling directly, I want to show you how to achieve success. So, let's take a look at how to sell on one of the biggest online auction sites and marketplaces which will connect you directly with buyers. I am talking, of course, about eBay.

eBay

eBay is the monarch of online platforms that facilitates the sale of goods between buyers and sellers. It is a very broad all-rounder in terms of what you can sell and it has 135 million active users, worldwide. What this means is that 135 million people have bought something on this site over the last 12 months. There are around 1.7 billion listings on eBay, which is more than 12 times the number of buyers. This means that to succeed you will have to stand out.

As I mentioned, you can sell most things on this platform

but below is a list of items I find reasonably easy to sell and turn a profit on this site:

> Electronics

> DVDs and CDs

> Books

> Mobile phones and accessories

> Computer games

> General clothing

> Children's toys and clothes

> Sports equipment

> Tools

> Watches – but for any worth over £3,000, I would use a specialist site. One of my favourites is watch-collecting.com

To succeed in being a great seller on eBay (or any sales site to be honest) follow my top tips:

Become active

First off, you need an active profile to prove to people you are real and trustworthy. To do this, you will have to start by buying some goods. I appreciate I'm trying to show you how to sell, but in order to secure lucrative sales, you need ratings. Buying everyday items you need will build up these ratings; meanwhile, you can also sell some of your small items at competitive prices. You will not be able to start with your highest priced items from the outset, so get active on here as soon as you can and once you've built your profile, you'll be able to sell it all.

Look out for the special offer days and weekends

eBay is famous for offering incentives for you to sell at certain times of the year. When they do this, they waver their 12.8 per cent fee and just charge £1 per item, or they might knock a large percentage off their usual fee. If you have loads to sell, these incentives can really save you hundreds of pounds.

Play the long game

Auction durations can be set for 3, 5, 7 or 10 days. I believe it's best to let the auction run as long as possible in order to generate the most interest. Also, plan for the auction to finish on a weekend day in the early evening, as this is when the most users are online bidding.

Start low to aim high

You can of course set a buy-now price on your item, but I prefer the auction route. It's always best to put your starting price low – entice people in with the lowest cost you can accept and it will generally generate a lot more bids.

Dan's Top Tip

Starting low to aim high is a good approach for general items. Anything niche or worth a significant amount of money should be priced accordingly, and I often suggest putting a reserve on such items to ensure it doesn't sell for below the profitable price.

In my experience at auctions, those items starting at a low point always get the most interest and make more money as a result.

The title is key

You have 80 characters to ensure you attract bidders/buyers to your item, so make them count. Each keyword will have an impact on how high or low you will appear in the list of results when people are searching. eBay's algorithm is designed to match customers with the most appropriate items based on their input. Generic terms like 'lovely' or 'attractive' are going to mass group you within the 1.7 billion items being sold at any one time, so you need get creative and use words specific to your item, its description and how buyers might search for it.

For example, if I'm selling a shirt, I will write:

Reiss Red and blue striped cotton men's shirt size medium

What I am doing with my keywords is giving the unique features most people will use when searching for a men's shirt. The brand, colour, material and size are all words any buyer will input to find a particular item of clothing.

If you need some guidance on this, search for items similar to yours that have already sold on the site and look at the keywords they used.

Here's my easy checklist to follow when creating a listing for something on this site:

☐ Check your spellings and grammar. Any mistakes will result in your appearing in fewer searches.

☐ Brands are a great keyword, so always include them if you're selling branded goods.

☐ Use factual words in your descriptions as this is what people will search for, rather than emotive words.

☐ Make use of the 80 characters available.

☐ Read and follow all the rules and regulations that eBay request you adhere too in order to be a valuable member of this community.

☐ Put the most important keywords at the start of the title to attract the eye of the buyer.

There are so many other sites you can sell on; some are less broad than eBay so can really benefit if you have a specific type of item to sell.

Etsy

I must admit that I do love the type of items that you can find on Etsy. It's great for homemade crafts and vintage items, particularly vintage jewellery that you may only get the scrap price for at your local jewellers or pawnbrokers. Items like this could be overlooked on eBay but will be loved and cherished by a vintage lover from any corner of the world. The great thing about Etsy is that there are 40 million buyers and only 2 million sellers, so if you have an item that is a little different and priced appropriately you should generate interest. The best way to understand this site is to go online and check out their 'popular right now' section.

If you have loads of vintage items or if you are a craftsperson who makes beautiful bespoke items then you will do well on this site. Some of the vintage items that sell well on Etsy include but are not limited to:

> Vintage clothes

> Kitchenware, such as Pyrex and old-school equipment like traditional weighing scales

> Jewellery – especially Victorian and Edwardian era

> Vintage furniture like desks, rugs and besides tables

There are some really strong free sites you can use too which have wonderful communities:

Gumtree

This really broad all-rounder is long established and trusted by many. Boasting over 8 million visitors to its site every month, it's one of the biggest of its kind. The whole process of advertising on this site is straightforward; it's easy to list items and you will no doubt get a lot of interest – although, as with all free sites, expect some haggling. Whilst it is an all-rounder, furniture and larger items tend to work well here, as does fitness equipment, outdoor items, clothing and sports equipment.

Other sites to check out

> Facebook Marketplace and groups is good if you want to sell things quickly and locally, so you don't have to mess around posting.

> Preloved is great for general household items. This platform has grown quite quickly over the past few

years and currently has around 10 million users,
so is very popular. The site is free to use but it does
offer two options to upgrade which have various
advantages for you as a seller. There is the full
option which is £6 annually or the premium which is
£18 annually.

> Shpock for me is like all the excitement and fun of
a car boot sale without having to leave your home.
With over 12 million users, this site is massive and
has a legion of loyal fans. This digital version of a car
boot sells everything you'd usually find at the Great
British tradition. You'll learn later how much of a fan
I am of the real-life hustle and bustle of an in-person
car boot, but this site is great for those of us short on
time and you can pretty much flog anything here at
any time of day.

Other ways to make sure you stand out in a crowded marketplace

> Always be honest. It pays to be truthful. Point out
the faults and issues with anything you sell. Do this
and it won't bite you on the bum later down the line
when it will undoubtedly be noticed and brought to
your attention.

> Your description matters. Just like we discussed
with the importance of the eBay title, the general
description is just as important and could help
keep a potential client interested and on the hook.
Always be clear, concise and informative with your
description and remember that buyers are well

versed on these sites so feel free to use their lingo – VGC means very good condition and BNIB means brand new in box. If you are unfamiliar with this terminology, a simple online search for ecommerce acronyms will deliver you a guide to popular abbreviations known within these communities.

> Always include the brand, the model, the condition, dimensions, colours, style and any other technical information, even if you have touched on it in the title. Remember to always re-read your listing before you make it live as misspellings can drop you from hundreds of searches.

> If in doubt, look at other top sellers on various sites to help get inspiration and see how they describe things in order to secure sales. After all, imitation is the sincerest form of flattery.

> Make it picture perfect. The more pictures you can upload the better. Selling in the digital space is a wonderful new way to make money but people want to be assured that the item they are purchasing is what they want, so you need to show them as many photos and angles of the objects as possible. Don't forget to take your pictures in good lighting with clear and clean backgrounds for clarity.

> Customer service is crucial. Always reply to emails as promptly as possible, be courteous and answer any questions with as much detail as possible. Dispatch as quickly as you can and do the little extras like sending an email when an item has been posted. I even put a little thank you note in with my sales.

These tiny additions cost so little but mean a lot. You are only as successful as your reputation, so customers who are satisfied with the entire sales process with you are more likely to leave you a positive review that others will read. They are also more likely to become a repeat customer.

> Be prepared to offer refunds. We don't always decide to keep the items we have bought, and this is the same with second-hand items. Be prepared for people wanting to return goods and receive a refund. Selling online is notorious for this and you don't want to risk damaging your reputation for being difficult during this process.

Selling on these sites is an easy and efficient way to make money, but don't forget a few last-minute checks:

Postage and packaging

You always need to include any costs you are going to incur for packaging and posting your goods. Make sure you work this out precisely before advertising your item(s). If you are lucky enough that your item will fit in a large envelope, then your costs will be reduced dramatically. Remember, if the P&P is cheaper for the customer then it's more likely to bag you a sale.

If there's no risk that the item will be damaged, try to make the package small enough to post at the cheapest option. If the item you've sold is cheap, don't worry too much about what you use to post the item in as the saving ultimately makes it cheaper for the customer. For more expensive items, consider including a gift-wrapping service for free. This doesn't have to be overly complicated and could just mean wrapping items in brown paper and tying a string bow to give a more professional feel.

And finally . . .

My last piece of advice with online sales is to be careful. I wish I didn't have to say this, but the harsh reality is that there are many scams associated with selling online and as we develop the digital landscape, these scammers continue to find new ways to get your goods. To help you not be a victim of one of these scams:

> Always look at a buyer's reviews. Scammers won't have reviews and if they do, they will not be positive. If a customer appears to be a little difficult you don't have to work with them.

> Send packages recorded delivery. Many scams involve the scammers telling sites that they haven't received the goods.

> Only accept payments through the sites' approved methods.

> Don't post anything until the payment has been received and cleared.

Auction houses

The other way you can sell direct to buyers but with the benefit of some specialist expertise is to go to an auction house. An auction house is the same as any of the online auctions you participate in: you will be charged a fee for using the service, but you will only make the money if the item sells, as opposed to the reseller/dealer method which guarantees you money as soon as they accept an item.

There are over 2,000 auction houses in the UK so look around to find one or even a couple that seem to sell similar items to what you have. I love an auction and have a wonderful relationship with some of the best auction houses in the UK – but be prepared, whilst some are more particular about the lots they will sell, others will try their hand with most goods. If you have auction houses local to you, get in touch as most will be happy to talk through how they can help and give you realistic advice and pricing on your belongings.

Resellers

If, however, you are keen to turn a quick profit, using dealers/resellers is a super-efficient way to get some extra money in your pocket without having to do any of the work.

This can be done online or in person.

In person

Pawnbrokers are a great resource to take your electricals, jewellery, art, antiques, watches, memorabilia, books and loads more. Walk down your local high street and pop into one to see what items they sell and discuss what you have. I specialise in jewellery, coins and watches, but have been known to take various other items over the years.

Antique dealers are also a great place to sell any of your old items. Whilst they are similar to pawnbrokers, if you have a very niche item, they may be better suited to help you sell it.

JACKPOT IN YOUR HIDDEN TREASURES

Online resellers

This is one of the fastest growing digital economies. Many companies saw that demand for earning extra cash from second-hand items was great but that ability to offer the time to do this yourself was limited.

As discussed, you take a hit on the price you will obtain using these because they are taking the risk and putting in the effort to sell your items, but this does put money in your pocket quickly and with less work. A lot of these sites operate within categories and some are more general:

> Books – Webuybooks.co.uk

> Vintage and antiques – Vintagecashcow.com

> General items – Ziffit.com or Textstuff.uk

> Music and computer goods – musicmagpie.co.uk

> Mobiles – mazumamobile.com or Fonebank.com

There is a relatively new platform called stuffusell.co.uk which sells on eBay for you but does all the work we talked about above. This comes at a premium of 35 per cent of the sale value, but if you have no time or idea how to do this for yourself, it can be a good option. (Although, you could always just re-read my advice about selling on eBay to make you a pro instead!)

Whichever way you decide to sell, there is a jackpot to be found in your hidden treasure, so get clearing your home and making money from your unwanted items right now.

RENT YOUR LIFE
FOR A PRICE

Viva la révolution! That's right, we are in the midst of one – a rental revolution. Throughout the world, something truly extraordinary is happening: there is a fascinating change in attitudes towards our possessions. Although 'generation rent' is used to describe an increasing number of people renting rather than owning homes, I want to reclaim it as the most exciting, new, sustainable, community-friendly method of unlocking extra cash from what we already have. Oh, and did I mention that renting out your items has the potential to earn you thousands of pounds a month? I thought you might like that.

If you need a cash injection fast, the simplest option can be to sell items you own, but could you be losing thousands of pounds opting for a quick result when the rental alternative could be a longer term and more regular financial solution?

The throwaway culture of the noughties is finally making way for a move to a sustainable, multi-use mindset, with rent, re-use and repurpose at its core. In this exciting new world, it's not only big ticket items like cars and homes we can rent; there is huge value to be unlocked in almost everything you own. What fascinates me with this mindset is the strengthening of community as a result. We are learning to trade with one another, capitalise on our assets and rent between each other.

In this chapter, I'm going to show you how to turn items you own into hard cash, in the most efficient and easy way – and it can be a lot of fun! I'll explain how pretty much everything in your home and bubble can be utilised and transformed into a money-making asset.

Renting everyday items is becoming the norm. A recent survey by *Which?* suggested that 88 per cent of people believe in renting their belongings – which is a staggering 55 per cent increase compared with five years ago. Consumerism is changing and, as we become more eco conscious, this rental trend marks a long-term shift in the way we consume products and make money from them.

As a society, we understand the damage that is being done to the planet; mass production of single-use plastics and electronic waste – exacerbated by planned obsolescence by manufacturers – are amongst the major factors contributing to global warming. As we become better informed about our choices and how they impact the environment around us, we know being sustainable is the only way forward.

Renting things we need helps the planet – and sharing what we have with others facilitates this, whilst making those items we have already spent money on release the cash we all need. According to Confused.com, Brits could earn up to £4,000 a month renting out items that belong to them.[5] But here is the best part – the part so simple yet so beautiful – that potential £4,000 is not a one-off, it's a regular cash stream that can continue month after month. Below is their most recent research into the average cost you can charge per rental of everyday items:

> Designer dress £255.50

> Marquee £252.50

> Speaker system £201

> Campervan £187.50

> Drone £141

> Designer suit £140

> Projector £114

> Laptop £101

> Camera £88.50

> Bike £88.50

> Amplifier £81

> Camera lens £58.50

> DJ deck £52.50

> Guitar £51.50

> Electric keyboard (musical) £51

> Microphone £36

> Electric scooter £32.50

> Tent £20

> Designer bag £17.50

> Sewing machine £16

> Drum pad £15.50

> Marquee heater £14.50

> Sleeping bag £8.50

As with all things in life, there are pros and cons to renting:

Pros:

> Can deliver regular cash injections

> You retain ownership of the item

> You'll make considerably more renting over a one-off payment you'd receive from selling.

Cons:

> The item could be damaged

> elling can provide a larger cash injection (but this is a one-off)

> Changes in market value and age of items can reduce rent ability and earning potential

> Time consuming to manage

If you like the sound of extra money in your pocket and you have assets to rent, let's start looking into the specifics. In this chapter, I will cover renting out:

1. Your wardrobe

2. Tools and gardening equipment

3. Your technology

4. Your bikes

Whilst some of you may not be able to rent these, I will also include renting out:

1. Your spare room(s) to people to live in

2. Your spare room(s) and other areas in your home for other purposes

Let's face it, short of renting your grandma – and I think that used to be a thing – the list of items you can rent is endless, so by having the tools and resources to understand how to harness your rental potential, you will be able to replicate this across other items you want to rent from your bubble.

Rent out your wardrobe

How many of us have clothes in drawers and in our wardrobes gathering dust, that have hardly been worn – even some that have never been worn (I am guilty of this) – taking up space and doing nothing for you? What I am about to tell you is pretty shocking and a sad hangover from our fast fashion past.

As a nation, we have over £30 billion of unwanted clothes just lying around in our wardrobes – that equates to around £500 per adult in the UK. Another shocking fact: 350,000 tonnes of clothes end up in landfill every year – worth, roughly, £12 billion.

Now, you could sell all of your unused clothes if you want a quick cash injection – I would never turn my back on selling, it's the core of my business – however, if you want a more regular stream of cash over a longer term, or perhaps you have an emotional attachment to some of your items, renting them could be just the answer.

The clothes rental sector hasn't just grown over the past few years, it's exploded! Rental fashion isn't just on the rise, it's a complete societal shift in how we live. It is estimated that the UK clothing rental market will be worth a meteoric £2.3 billion by 2029.

Why the change, you ask? Various reasons – the ever-increasing cost of clothes, inflation, stagnation in wages and, of course, our awareness that we have to be sustainable. Our addiction to fast and cheap fashion created a throwaway mindset but renting is the ultimate cure.

So, what can you rent out of your wardrobe and how much could you earn? Firstly, you need to look at this with a degree of common sense – bargain items you purchased are unlikely to bring you any return. You need to understand the market and opportunity. People are renting to make fashion more sustainable and affordable – why spend £150 on a dress you might wear to one event when you could rent it for £30? If it's good enough for the likes of Holly Willoughby, Stacey Dooley and Laura Whitmore, it's good enough for us.

What and how you rent comes down to how much disposable time you have on your hands. Operating a rental fashion business can be lucrative whatever the cost of your clothes, but your pricing will have to match. For instance, if you want to rent a pretty blouse you purchased for £40, there is definitely a market for it, but you'll have to set a realistic rental cost – roughly 10 per cent of the purchase price (£4) – and therefore will need to rent this more often to make serious cash. But if, on the other hand, you have an evening gown purchased for £450, this could be rented for £69 per time. Remember, rental fashion isn't just for special occasions, people rent clothes for the everyday – date nights, job interviews, weekends away or just to look good for a night out with friends.

If you're fortunate enough to have designer items, there is a big market for these, as people who may never be able to buy still want to try. So, anything from designer handbags, sunglasses, ball gowns and even wedding dresses enjoy huge demand within rental fashion.

What you charge to rent out your wardrobe also depends greatly on market needs. You don't have to be Einstein to realise that your heat-retaining puffer jacket probably isn't going to do well for you in the summer months.

When setting a price for your wardrobe, do your research, look at your competitors and what they are offering. Then take into consideration the material, style brand of your items and market them with realistic values. As with all markets, there will be fluctuation as supply and demand changes, so keep an eye on trends to target which parts of your wardrobe will make you the most at various times throughout the year.

As I mentioned above, as a general rule of thumb, you should rent your items for 10–20 per cent of the price you paid for it. That would mean you could cover the entire cost you paid for one item within 5–10 rentals and everything after that is pure profit (after costs). Isn't it amazing to think we live in a world where we can effectively get clothes for free and actually earn money from them? Not only can your clothes pay for themselves but when you are in profit they can start paying towards your monthly outgoings or starting a holiday fund and so much more.

There are many reputable fashion rental platforms on the market for you to choose from. They all charge various levels of commission, depending on how much you want them to do for you.

For example, My Wardrobe HQ manages the whole process from start (photography) to end (return clothes), but they take 40 per cent of the rental price. This sounds like a lot, but if you are time poor then 60 per cent of the rental revenue for doing nothing is not bad and it's certainly a lot more than an item is making you at the back of your wardrobe.

But if you just want the advantage of using a platform with an established client base, you're generally looking at an average of 15 per cent commission. Some of these will also offer other assurances for you, like comprehensive policies to ensure damaged clothes are fixed, replaced or fully paid for. Accidents happen and, in most cases, it may be a spilt drink or a lost button, but if your items don't get returned or are damaged beyond repair the platform you're using and the policy you have in place means you will be suitably reimbursed. All policies and terms and conditions differ, so do your due diligence and check you're getting the right level of cover for your items and anything you may be liable for.

In order to market your clothes, you will need to take great pictures of them – believe me, taking pictures of your clothing is serious business; I don't want to see any clothes hanging precariously from the wardrobe door!

Sell the dream of your item – stand out from the crowd, look professional and make the clothes pop and feel attainable yet desirable. The key is not to complicate things. Below are some of my personal tips and tricks to succeed – lights, camera . . . action:

> Get the lighting right. You can invest in ring lights and other fancy lighting like LED panels but I'm here to teach you how to make money not spend it! Whilst we're being sustainable let's use Mother Nature – I think everything looks better in natural light. Find a spot outside and use this for all your photos so you have a uniform brand. To get what I call the 'good light' you want to be taking your pictures between 8am and 10am.

> Choose the right equipment. Most smart phones have HD/4K quality these days but if you have a camera, feel free to use that. I know I said not to buy above but I advise getting yourself a cheap tripod to get clear, non-shaky pictures.

> Prepare the clothes. Make sure to iron out any creases and remove any lint – people know you are renting them but they'll be attracted if the clothes look like new.

> Pick the right background. Keep it neutral and not distracting. You can always apply a filter to mask the background if you're struggling.

Now it's time to shoot to impress:

> Shoot yourself wearing the clothes as this helps sell the dream of what they look like on and is my preferred method.

> ❯ If you have a mannequin, you could use that. Just make sure the item fits. If it's too big, use the trick of clipping the item from behind to give a more fitted illusion.

> ❯ There's nothing wrong with hanging the clothing on a clothes hanger, just make sure you can see how the item looks in full.

> ❯ Some people opt to lay their items flat, but this can often look one-dimensional and, as you're outside, could get quite messy!

Pictures say a thousand words, but the description you give an item is also really important. The more information you can supply on the site, the sooner your item can be making you money. Give all the details – type of fabric, colour(s), size, key measurements, feel to the touch, number of pockets/zips, formal or everyday wear. Offering all the information upfront stops you getting caught in lengthy correspondence.

On occasion people will still have questions, so make sure you are responsive. You shouldn't be on your phone or computer constantly (this is not good for you), but in a digital world where we are used to communicating instantly, customers will often have questions and expect answers quickly and if you're slow to respond you risk losing potential return customers.

When choosing which platform to use, look at offerings like push notifications, so that you know when someone is asking a question. Or clearly advertise that you reply to questions at a set time of day due to life commitments. Being transparent often helps retain a loyal client base.

Where possible, I always like to reply to a prospective client within two hours of a question being asked (providing it's not overnight and I'm asleep). The maximum time you should take to respond to someone is 24 hours – but I'd say you'll have lost your client by this time.

There are loads of outstanding rental fashion sites, such as Hirestreet and Cocoon. Below I've picked a couple to show you the sort of things you'll be asked for and what you get in return:

Hurr collective

One of the most recognised and reputable platforms on the market is Hurr collective, who also have a pop-up boutique in Selfridges – fancy! To use them, the criteria is simple: your clothes most be under two years of age and have a recommended retail price of £120 and over. In return, they reckon you will earn your initial outlay within four to five rentals. As I mentioned in the opening, after this you are having a pure profit party!

They offer insurance which covers any minor damage up to £50 and any major damage will result in the renter paying the full RRP. You can also charge the renter a cleaning fee on top of the rental price. Rental periods can be set for 4, 8, 10 or 20 days. The return postage is paid by the renter; there is a £25 a day late rental fee – but be aware, if the item doesn't fit the renter, they don't have to pay.

Hurr takes a 12 per cent commission on your charges.

By Rotation

The OG when it comes to rental fashion – By Rotation launched the world's first social fashion rental app in 2019. It's a peer-to-peer platform that includes a resale function. Their aim is to make fashion circular and accessible – with 60,000 items available to rent, they're making a good start.

I love the way you can navigate around their site and choose categories ranging from ski wear, dresses, wedding dress and black tie. It's fresh and fun and the categories are interesting. It has an appeal that is multi-generational.

This site encourages renters and lenders to resolve disputes regarding loss, theft or damage directly. But, if the item isn't returned or is damaged beyond repair, the renter can be charged the market value for the item. Always report any damage straight away and as with all sites, make sure you read each company's terms and conditions.

Rental periods can be anything from one day upwards, and return postage is paid by the renter with late fees set by the lender. Unlike Hurr, if it doesn't fit the renter, you still get paid. By Rotation takes a 15 per cent commission on your charges.

Whichever platform you choose to rent your items through, always check:

> Size and market performance

> Satisfaction rating customers give the site

> What cover they offer for damages to your items

> Who covers cleaning of the item

> Rental periods

> Dispute and resolution protocol

Whatever you do, do not ever use a website/platform that doesn't offer assurances or money back if your item is damaged or not returned. I have come across horror stories where people have tried to avoid paying commission to a reputable company and have no contract or terms and conditions in place. Any issues will have to be taken up by you and its unlikely you'll succeed with a satisfactory resolution.

Lastly, before we move on to my next category I want to give my final bit of fashion rental advice – weddings! If you've been married, your wedding outfit is one of the biggest financial investments you will have undertaken. Sixty per cent of brides keep their dresses and yet only 7 per cent rent them out. There is money to be made in your wedding outfit – on average, you can rent a wedding dress or suit for £50–£200 per day (more for designer). Carrie Johnson rented her wedding dress for her marriage to the former PM. It is an untapped market with huge earning potential.

Rent out your tools and gardening equipment

I bet you didn't know that Brits have £2 billion of tools that are rarely used and that, as a nation, we spend £20 billion a year on new tools. These figures are eye-watering – if there are so many unused tools out there, there should be no need to buy new. Supposedly, the average power tool is used for somewhere between six and twenty minutes in its entire lifetime. Demand for tools and gardening equipment is evident, which is why the rental market for these items is fast becoming big business.

As people realise they don't need to own or if finances determine they can't afford to own, renting is a method which helps all – less mass production impacting the environment, feasible opportunity to help people with financial difficulty and a real opportunity to make money from your belongings.

Fat Llama (a rental site not a chubby member of the camel family) enables people to rent almost anything locally. It's a fantastic opportunity for you to make money from your equipment – with little to no overheads and only commission you should be earning decent money in no time.

Here's a list of everyday tools and what you could potentially earn in rental from them:

> Snap-on screwdriver set ×12 – £10 per day

> Handsaw – £2 per day

> Step ladder (8 steps) – £12 per day

> Extension cable with three plug sockets – £3 per day

> Hedge trimmer – £12 per day

> Garden strimmer – £8 per day

> Garden shovel – £4 per day

> Lawn mower – £15 per day

At first glance, it is apparent that these figures aren't going to get you onto that beach for early retirement any time soon, but these items will get you cash quickly and relatively easily. You can advertise your tools on a rental site and have customers come to you, collect the items and then return them. It's easy profit and it means things that generally sit on a shelf in your home are making good money for you.

Look at it this way, how often do you mow your lawn? At most, once a week – in my case, maybe less so – therefore, six days of the week your lawnmower is sat doing nothing. Making that asset earn its keep could make you tens of pounds a week, hundreds a year.

Writing this chapter made me have a look around my home and it is staggering the number of tools I have lying around gathering nothing but dust.

For instance, I have a cordless power drill – I have probably used it once – which could be earning me £10 a day. Even if I only rented it three times a month, it would make me £360 a year – the average amount one person would budget for spending money on a week-long holiday – all from one tool.

Use my handy list template on the next page to write down all the tools and garden equipment you own that could be making you money instantaneously. Then register with a reputable rental platform (like Fat Llama, MyShed app or RentMy) and watch the money start rolling in.

Gardening Tools

Tools	Rental price per day

Rent out your technology

Be honest with me, who has bought a piece of tech, used it for a few days and then forgotten about it as it collects dust on a shelf or in a drawer? I certainly have. In fact, 61 per cent of us own laptops yet 42 per cent of us claim that we don't use them very often. A sobering thought when we consider that the laptop you rarely use could currently be making you anything from £7 to £50 (model dependent) per day!

Renting tech is on the rise, not only because it is more sustainable for the planet but because it is evolving so quickly – you can buy a new phone today and the next day the same brand has released a new model. I think only people in the top 1 per cent of earners could upgrade that often, but even if you were in the top 1 per cent would you really do that anyway?

Renting tech benefits everyone by giving access to unused goods and potentially, in the long run, slowing down mass production and stopping throw-away culture.

Generally we don't need tech 24/7. For example, a student will have access to a computer in school but may benefit from the use of a laptop at home for a couple of days to finish coursework. You might have a laptop or computer at home for those occasions you work from home but it isn't used daily. So with careful planning you can optimise that tech to make money for you and help those around you.

Time is of the essence when it comes to technology as this category evolves so quickly. In most circumstances, the older the tech the less valuable it will be when it comes to the rental market. So, if you intend to make money from your tech, my advice is to do it as soon as you get it.

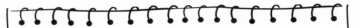

Dan's Top Tip

Remember when renting any technology, restore each device to factory settings and remove any personal information.

This doesn't mean that your five-year-old laptop can't be rented out, of course it can, but it won't achieve as much rental income as a newer version.

However, don't misread the opportunity of rental income from your tech as a new business venture. As each generation of tech improves on the last, the rate of progress from version to version speeds up. So my advice would only be to utilise the tech in your home your currently have, or tech you need to buy for a specific reason, as if you buy solely to rent, your tech will be outdated before you know it and it wouldn't be a sound investment.

The tech category is huge and it would probably take me an entire book to even scratch the surface, so here I'll just give you some headline categories and overviews to get you started and most of my advice should be transferable to various other forms of tech you may want to rent.

Some of the items I see doing really well in the tech rental space at the moment are:

> Laptops and computers

> Carpet cleaners

> Video game consoles

> Smartphones

> Sound system speakers

> Drones

> Electric barbecues

> Cameras

> Camera lenses

> DJ equipment

> Sewing machines

These are just a few of the items you may own that you use occasionally but can be making money for you when they are not in use.

The process of renting tech is relatively simple, so below is a quick checklist to get you up and renting:

CHECKLIST

☐ Find the best platform to rent your tech (examples below).

☐ Create a profile on the platform using your social media account or email.

☐ Choose an accessible username and, if the platform allows, upload a picture of yourself – this makes your account personable and trustworthy. I'm much more likely to rent tech from 'Richard' with a profile picture than I would of 'justageek27' without a pic.

☐ State clearly what tech you have to rent and give the specifics – make, model, age and anything else that will make it attractive to potential renters.

☐ Upload loads of pictures of the item to show what condition it is in.

☐ Set your location.

☐ Advertise your rental price (as always, do your research for this beforehand so that you don't price yourself out of the market).

☐ As always, read the T&Cs and small print, make sure any insurance/protection the company offers covers you for every eventuality.

Below are two different platforms where you can try to rent your tech (but there are many more):

Fat Llama

With a name like this it's hard to forget this well-known platform. Fat Llama is the market leader in renting out your items and it's not just technology – their portfolio is vast and covers most things that you can find around your home. They are a one-stop shop, easy to sign up to and straightforward to deal with.

Fat Llama does have high rental fees, which is a charge of 25 per cent to you and 25 per cent to the person renting your item – so if you have an item to rent for £100, the renter pays £125, you receive £75. In black and white, this looks like a lot but this platform has a strong foothold in the market, plus they also offer so many guarantees and assurances to justify this cost – you get an owner guarantee to protect your items, which means the renter is liable if they break or damage your item, plus if the renter goes AWOL, Fat Llama will cover your item up to £25,000 of the value. They also have one of the most robust verifications systems on the market. There isn't a subscription fee so you only pay when you successfully rent an item.

RentMy

It may not be as prolific as some of the other platforms but RentMy lets you rent out most things from around your home. For me, the site is a little more complicated to navigate but once you've got past the clunkiness and done it a few times, listing items does become clearer.

RentMy have very competitive fees and may soon become more attractive to the renters, as they only charge the owner a fee of 20 per cent. At the time of writing, their presence in the rental market isn't as big as others, but I do think they will grow and develop into a strong platform as the rental revolution takes hold.

I like the verification process that this company offers as they check both renter and owner via ID and proof of address. They track all rental agreements and you are protected up to £15,000 if anything should happen to your items.

Rent out your bikes

The latest data regarding unused bikes in the UK is pretty mind blowing (what can I say, I love a fact). A study by the Bike Club reveals that there are around 38 million unused bikes in the UK.[6] This works out at around 34 per cent of the adult population who have a bike and simply don't use it. Don't worry, my maths hasn't gone off (I know there are over 66 million adults in the UK): of those 38 million bikes, 7.9 million adults have one unused child's bike and many have up to three. That could be around £360 million in lost revenue per month – now you see why my mind is blown!

Bike rental is going to be big business. Not only does it feed in to a general desire to be more sustainable, but with governments around the world looking to cut emissions, we are seeing the creation of pedestrian and cyclist only zones, cycle paths emerging on roads and a general move to discourage cars and encourage cycling. Clean air zones and congestion charges are being implemented in our major cities and this is fuelling the popularity of cycling. The benefits to many are plain to see: you save money, you help the environment and you get fit in the process.

I want you – as a bubble entrepreneur – to seize on this movement, dust down that bike and start to appreciate the money-making potential it may have. You don't even have to rent it out full time to make a decent income; you can do it on a part-time basis and still enjoy the many benefits of cycling yourself.

On average, the majority of bike rental platforms suggest a monthly income of between £400–£500. I dug a bit deeper and did some cross-platform research, looking at different makes and models of bikes, and I think you are likely to be able to charge £20–£40 per day. That means, if you were to rent out your bike 28 days a month then you could expect £560–£1,120 per month (minus fees, which we will get to later). That being said, if you own a bike you likely want to use it occasionally, so even on a more conservative estimate, if you rented your bike for 15–20 days a month, you could still be earning hundreds of pounds. Having spoken with many cyclists, demand is out there, so this market isn't going anywhere anytime soon.

To get yourself started, my usual rule applies – do your market research! Find out which platforms operate in your area and which of them has the biggest subscription base, takes the least commission and offers you the most assurances and protection should anything happen to you bike.

As with most rental, the set-up is pretty simple and foolproof if you follow my guidance:

> Choose the best platform for you and your area.

> Upload photos. Bikes that have clear photos rent out more frequently. Use natural light (I suggest 9am as a great time of day), a plain background and make sure your bike is spotlessly clean. Take loads of different angles of the bike in landscape.

> Write a title and description. I would include the make and model, its age and if you're including any extras such as helmet and locks. It's also useful to describe if your bike has any height restrictions. Remember, the more information you give here the less time wasted on back-and-forth questions with potential renters.

> Put the price per hour, day or week that you want. The best way to choose a realistic price is to look at what your model or a similar model is being rented out for elsewhere in your area. I would charge 5 per cent less than others are charging for a bike like yours to get started. You can always increase your prices when you have a regular stream of clients.

> Put the area where your bike can be collected from –

only share your full address privately after a booking is confirmed.

The majority of platforms allow you to have your bike continually listed. Once a request comes in, you can accept or decline depending on your availability.

It really is that simple and easy to earn some cash quickly – BUT always remember to check you have the right level of protection for you and your bike. I cannot stress this enough. Most platforms come with a vetting process to ensure you are renting to trusted and authentic people and they all come with insurance to cover your bike if the worst should happen – just make sure you read the small print for how much this insurance is for, as if your bike is worth more, you may need to shop around for another platform or even try your home insurance to see if you can cover the bike yourself for a rental purpose.

As renting becomes the norm, there are of course a multitude of platforms to choose from. Below I have reviewed two but also find the right one for your needs:

Spinlister

This platform is long established, and quick and easy to use. It allows people with bikes all around the world to connect with people who want to rent them. The process of signing up is pretty simple and uploading the details of your bike is straightforward. There are several safety nets in place that will put your mind at ease when it comes to renting, such as the Spinlister guarantee – which offers damage protection on your bike up to £800. You also have simple yet effective verification processes in place that use social media and credit card company tools to make sure the person you are renting your bike to really is the person who they say they are. Listings are free and you are charged a 17.5 per cent fee of your rental price. This isn't the lowest I have seen, however, for the exposure it will give your bike through the site's international audience and the checks and assurances they give you, I feel this fee is worth it.

ListnRide

I found this platform a little frustrating to navigate at times but they have a lot of helpful content on their site to get you on the right track when it comes to renting out your bike. I like the fact that this site makes you feel like you are part of a community and, once I worked out how to list, I enjoyed interacting with the platform. The service fee for the lister ranges between 10 and 15 per cent. They also include various assurances and insurance policies, so check if they work for your needs.

Deciding which company to use is up to you, but as I mentioned at the beginning – do your research! Look at testimonials from real people who explain how easy or difficult the process was, whether they were renting what was advertised (make, model and condition) and look at the reach and the community who engage with the platform. If you can, speak to others who rent on the platform already and remember that each will have a different way of paying you. Whether PayPal, BACS transfer or direct, check you are set up to receive your funds and also check how much of a lag there is from rental to payment – some platforms offer payment straight after the rental period; others have a hold back.

Whatever you do, do not try to rent your bike yourself. It may be appealing to just pop it up on social media but this is risky business. Remember that platforms charging you a fee are doing so because they have real costs to check people are who they say they are and that your bike is covered for any eventuality. If you go it alone you have no assurances and to chase any late payments or damage, you will have to go through lengthy (and costly) court proceedings.

Renting out your spare room(s) to people

According to latest research, 18.6 million bedrooms lie empty in the UK, making it one of the most obvious rental opportunities with the highest profit margin. Meanwhile, we need 145,000 affordable houses to be built every year to meet demand. The price of traditional hotels and B&Bs makes travel unaffordable for many. So why not connect these empty rooms with the people who need them, on a short- or long-term basis, and let your spare room earn money for you?

Over 1 billion stays have been booked through rental provider, AirBnB, so it's no surprise when they reported that demand outstrips supply. Worldwide, Airbnb is seeing impressive figures being reported for rentals. Plus Airbnbs are often in better locations without the sterile touch of what can be soulless and generic hotel chains.

Airbnb is controversial within the wider housing crisis of the UK. In the late 1990s and during the early part of the twenty-first century, 'buy to let' mortgages were offered widely, creating a large rise in the number of largely unregulated private landlords renting properties to tenants. As Airbnb grew quickly and exponentially, these landlords realised they could earn on average 30 per cent more renting their properties on a short-term basis to tourists or business travellers than to long-term tenants. This has led to skyrocketing rents, particularly in cities or in tourist destinations like Cornwall, which is now unaffordable for people who live there, who have to compete with visitors prepared to pay £1,000 for a week in a two-bed cottage. Clearly there needs to be regulation in this sector.

However, renting out a bedroom which would otherwise be often empty – maybe it's a guest room, storeroom, unused gym room – provides a real, needed service without having so much impact on the general rental market.

Alternatively, you can rent out your room on a long-term basis – taking lodgers is nothing new – as it offers you financial stability for a longer period if you are happy to make the commitment of having someone else in your home for an extended period of time. This way, you can interview the tenant thoroughly and find someone who is a great match for your household (ensure you have the right to sub-let in your leasehold agreement and that it doesn't impact or invalidate any insurance policies). Since Victorian and Edwardian industrialisation, lodgers have been a staple fixture for families who are struggling with bills and workers who have a wage but need a room to rent. It was, and continues to be, a win–win situation.

However, short-term room rental is a relatively new phenomenon facilitated by technology. It is feasible for many people who need access to their spare room some of the time or who do not want an additional household member all the time.

If you are happy with the risk of fluctuating income associated with short-term rentals, as opposed to the guaranteed, contracted income of a long-term tenancy agreement, you could rent out your spare room for as much as four or five times more per night than you could charge on a longer term basis. Short-term rental also offers you more flexibility; you can rent when on holiday, only offer rental on weekdays so you have the weekend to yourself or maybe even just consider it for January when money is a bit tight if you are suffering from a Christmas financial hangover.

Airbnb is one of the most highly regarded and successful platforms that can enable you to rent out your spare room with ease. The whole process is quick, simple and can see you earning money almost instantly. In fact, Airbnb has stated that, on average, new hosts secure bookings within the first five days of listing.

The average you can expect to earn is around £70 per night for your spare room through a rental platform. So, imagine doing this just three days a week for a year. Based on the average rate of £70 per night, multiplied by the 156 days a year you rent, you could, minus the 3 per cent Airbnb commission, be taking home an additional £10,592 per year. This is a money tap you can turn on and off depending on your financial situation in any given month.

Even an occasional host could earn the equivalent of two months' salary extra per year, based on recent data revealed by Airbnb.

There are multiple platforms that can help you rent out your room but the small commission has made Airbnb a highly attractive option. So for my case study, I will use Airbnb to explain how you can rent your spare room safely and securely.

Like any other business, you'll need to invest your time, effort and sometimes some money to make your rental journey pay off. There are profits to be made if you follow a strategy and have a clear plan.

Below, I give you the tips and tricks to do this properly,

effectively and with the opportunity for big rewards.

Basic facts

Airbnb charges you 3 per cent of the net value – in simple terms, the total amount you want to charge for the rental, they will take 3 per cent of that figure. So if you charge £100 a night, AirBnB take £3, leaving you with £97 earned before deducting any operating costs (cleaning, supplies, heating, hot water, electricity, broadband and anything else you will offer guests).

The site takes care of marketing, brand awareness and the legal T&Cs – this is likely going to release profit from your asset much more quickly than you could manage on your own, and, let's face it, it's a small price to pay for partnering up with the biggest short-term rental platform on the planet.

Now for the detail

First, make sure you are properly insured – after all, this is your home. Always consult your personal insurance provider to ensure renting your spare room doesn't invalidate any buildings or contents insurance you may have.

Airbnb offer something called Aircover. This service is always included and always free. It includes:

> Guest verification to check names, addresses and government-issued ID.

> Reservation screening, which is a technological analysis that looks at hundreds of factors in each reservation and will block certain bookings that show a high risk for disruptive parties and property damage.

> $3 million damage protection in regards to art and valuables, vehicle(s), pet damage and income loss.

> Cover for extra cleaning services outside the standard T&Cs.

> Cover for $1 million if a guest injures themselves whilst staying at your property.

Now, get your calendar in order. I know this is a reoccurring theme through all my top tips and tricks, but I'll say it again: maintaining an up-to-date calendar is essential. Time really is money and dealing with a double booking or chaotic scheduling is going to cause headaches for all parties. So ensure your calendar has all the bookings recorded, or you have clearly noted the times when you don't want to rent it out at all. For instance, if you haven't blocked out Christmas when you are expecting just family and friends, and then have to cancel on someone who thought they had a place to stay for the festive season, not only will you lose cash but also your reputation – you are only as profitable as your last review.

Also mark key dates associated with your area. Local events, festivals and celebratory seasons like Easter and summer holidays are the key times at which demand is high and you can charge a premium.

If you target your rental calendar around local events, you could earn a third more for a third less time people are in your home. Therefore, the cost of hosting goes down and your profit goes up, resulting in you working smarter for your money rather than harder.

Bear in mind that pricing your rental room isn't as easy as just copying what your competitors will charge. You need to assess what you are offering and how to make it the most attractive to generate regular bookings. Know your pricing strategy, and remember that with the UK government's rent a room scheme you can earn £7,500 per year tax free.

Now let's look at what you need to factor in when looking at your costs and deciding your rates.

What are your daily operating costs?

As a general rule, I would take a look at how much it costs to run your home (minus food) per month and divide that figure by the days within that month. So add your monthly rent/mortgage plus your average heating, water and electricity to your council tax bill and any other additional charges, such as insurance, then divide that total by the amount of days in a month. This is your minimum daily operating cost.

What could increase your daily operating costs?

Are you going to offer anything additional to stand out in a thriving market? Things like bathroom supplies, laundry detergent, coffee and tea, breakfast . . . All of these extras may seem small but over the course of a year they can stack up. So add these to your minimum daily operating cost.

Time to become a detective . . .

Doing your market research is key. Setting your rental price too high or too low both have negative impacts – too high, people can find something cheaper in your area. Too low, people worry they are sleeping in your kitchen cupboard. So be price-savvy and cushion yourself in the sweet spot.

Go online and conduct multiple searches within your local area, selecting filters that are applicable to what you will eventually be offering. When you've found some like-for-like offerings, you can get an understanding of the different rates you can charge for various days of the week and times of the year – this is your sweet spot.

Be flexible

You know your actual operating cost, and you know your sweet spot, so now you need to work out your flexible pricing strategy. Applying a one-size-fits-all pricing plan for the 365 days of the year could ultimately cost you thousands of pounds in earning potential.

Changes in market demand, often affected by geographical and societal events, means that you are better served to maximise your earning potential if you can be flexible. This isn't rocket science. Fewer people holiday in autumn and winter, but lots of people look for Christmas and New Year getaways, so set your prices lower for November and a couple of weeks of early December, then increase them for the seasonal period. Look at your local calendar for events – when is demand going to be high? If there is more demand than there is supply, you need to be shrewd and increase your pricing. Airbnb has a useful tool to help you set custom pricing for certain dates which you can clearly advertise on your online calendar.

Then there's the basics – you are going to get less on a Monday than you are on a Friday, so my top tip here is to work out what you want to earn in rent for a week, then divide that by seven. Take a little bit off the earlier days of the week and add what you've taken off to the weekend days you're renting. A rough rule of thumb: you should be charging 10–15 per cent more for more in demand days like weekends.

Incentivise people to stay longer

We all love a discount and you should not be afraid to reward people who are opting to stay longer – if that's something you would like to encourage, as longer stay equals more pay and cuts the work you put in to turnaround the room and welcome a new guest.

Offering a longer stay discount is clever because it doesn't make the renter suspect they'd be staying in your kitchen cupboard but instead is rewarding them for their loyalty. This also encourages repeat business for people who return to your area regularly.

For starters, I would offer a 10 per cent reduction in nightly rates for a booking of a week and a 20 per cent reduction for that of a month – but ALWAYS research your local area and similar offerings to make sure you are competitive within your market.

Profit potential

Now for the juicy bit . . . With your realistic daily operating cost determined, plus knowledge of the short-term rental pricing in your local area, you can now work out your nightly charges to have a clear understanding of your profit potential.

You need to add in a few other factors, like your time, cleaning and turnover (though you can charge extra for this) plus your initial set-up costs to launch. Airbnb might do the marketing and run the secure booking system, but you are going to have to be the welcoming host, perfecting your offerings and ensuring yours is the place where people want to stay. So this should all be reflected in your pricing strategy to ensure a healthy profit.

Make it rain . . . eventually

This is your new money-making venture and, let's be honest, you're renting out part of your home, so you should be rewarded – BUT you need to entice a client base.

One of my first tips with this is to offer a reduced rate to begin with. Enter the market with all the same offerings as your local competitors but at a 20 per cent reduction. Your initial profit margin will be lower (but still more than enough to cover real costs) whilst establishing you as a place to stay and more importantly, pay!

The digital revolution

When you have established yourself on the market, it is time to embrace the digital age. In order to be a short-term rental ruler, lay off doing everything manually and use one of the many automation tools that can help you manage your new money-making venture.

Tools like Host Tools collates all the information relating to your rental offering and works out the optimum you can charge throughout the year.

You know your price . . . what next?

Now that you have a pricing strategy, here are the final bits of preparation you'll need to tackle before you become a money-making, room-rental machine!

> ❯ Give yourself plenty of time to turn the room around from check-out to check-in. On average, a single bedroom shouldn't take longer than an hour to turn over, but you will need to schedule time to ensure the bathroom and toilet is in order – no short and curlies here please.

> I suggest having spare bedding and towels so that you're not faffing, trying to wash and dry these essentials between paying guests.

> Offer an attractive check in time – 3pm is quite standard and lets guests settle in before whatever plans they may have for the evening. If you schedule an 11am check out time, this is not only attractive as others often opt for a 10am check out time, but it also gives you four hours to turn around the room ready for the next guests.

> They say cash is king but I'll change that to knowledge is king! Create a 'check-in pack' which informs your paying guests of how the space they have rented works. This will include Wi-Fi accounts and passwords, instructions for heating or cooling the room, how the TV and any extras like Sky/Netflix, etc., work.

> Including the basics is a must for me, it's the little things that can make the biggest difference. So I would always include necessities like toiletries, tea, coffee, sugar, salt and pepper, etc. Here is a simple check in sheet template you can use to keep on top of this between guests:

CHECKLIST

- ☐ Remove all rubbish from room.
- ☐ Check no personal belongings have been left behind in cupboards, drawers under the bed etc.
- ☐ Change all bedding and towels.
- ☐ Vacuum floors and under bed.
- ☐ Dust and polish all surfaces like windowsills, ledges, sides, ornaments and mirrors.
- ☐ Check for general wear and tear.
- ☐ Make sure electrical goods are in working order.
- ☐ Ensure wardrobe has appropriate amount of hangers, spare blanket and pillows.
- ☐ Supply a fan in summer/hot months.
- ☐ Clean bathroom.
- ☐ Replenish toiletries, tea and coffee (if providing).

Anything additional you can do will always help you to stand out in a crowded market – get to know your guests before they arrive and find out why they are coming to stay. Whether it is for business or pleasure, understanding why they are in town can help you know what advice to offer them on restaurants, travel and local attractions. With this intel, you can add any recommendations to your check-in pack. Tailoring it to each guest – especially if they are staying for a few nights or more – takes less time than you think but makes each guest feel special and considered.

Aside from Airbnb, there are loads of platforms you can use to market and rent your spare room but unfortunately I can't advise you which is best suited for your needs. So do your research to find the one that will best help you make money from renting your spare room in the way that works best for you.

Below is a headline summary of some of the most well-known rental platforms:

VRBO

Established in 1995, this is the grandparent of 'rent out your room' platforms – it's highly regarded and now owned by Expedia.

Key points:

> Operates in 190 countries

> For entire home rental only

> Has a 5 per cent flat rate commission plus a 3 per cent payment processing fee

> Is a good platform for families to use

> Key screening and security cover included (but always read the terms and conditions)

Airbnb

Recognised as the rental market leader but, as discussed earlier, that doesn't always mean it is the best for your needs. This platform has over 150 million users worldwide.

Key points:

> Operates in 220 countries

> You can rent out your spare room or entire property

> Has a 3 per cent flat rate commission

> Perfect for single/short-term stays

> Impressive client-screening process and comprehensive cover (always read the small print)

Misterb&b

Established for the LGBTQ+ community, this is a fantastic site that has established a worldwide network for travellers from this community to find safe and friendly places to stay.

Key points:

> Operates in over 130 countries

> Charges host and guest fees calculated as a percentage of the booking

> You can rent a spare room or entire property

> 24-hour dedicated helpline

> You have full control over who you do and do not allow to rent

> Dedicated trust and safety department to ensure all users are who they say they are

Homestay

The emphasis with this platform is interaction with your guest. They sell their platform as offering an authentic experience and staying with a local.

Key points:

> Operates in over 160 countries

> ❭ Weekday rentals only

> ❭ Promotes sustainable local tourism

> ❭ Has a 3 per cent flat rate commission

Booking.com

This is a household name so putting your room on here could give it some extra clout. I'd say they are probably the closest competitor to Airbnb, but do they falter with a higher commission rate?

Key points:

> ❭ 15 per cent commission charged

> ❭ 1 billion customers annually

> ❭ Easy system that is simple to navigate

The DIY approach

Of course, there is the option not to use any of these platforms and to rent out your room entirely by yourself. The upside is that you take all the profit and don't have to use a third party, but renting out your room DIY style does involve a lot more hard work. If you have the time and inclination, your hard work can provide a profitable business venture.

The key with taking the DIY rental method is networking and community. You have to put the emphasis on local people helping locals, and this incorporates everything that I love about renting. This method also promotes sustainable tourism by encouraging money to be spent within your community, and by offering your facilities you are minimising your environmental impact.

The DIY approach isn't too dissimilar to the platform

approach outlined previously: you have to keep a comprehensive diary, offer a quality rental room and have a competitive pricing strategy in order to be successful. Remember, however, that the responsibility for securing renters lies entirely on your shoulders.

I must also raise the important fact that vetting potential renters is paramount for your safety and security, which is why I believe that my 'networking method' is the most secure if you are doing this alone. This method is pretty simple – in fact, unlike most things, I can summarise it in just one sentence: 'talk to businesses and organisations'.

By letting local organisations and businesses know that you have a room(s) for short-term rentals can guarantee you bookings pretty quickly. These companies will have also done the vetting for you, to give you a better sense of safety, and most will welcome your approach, so that they don't have to worry about finding accommodation or paying hefty hotel prices. There are a number of different sorts of companies that you can approach who will value being able to rent your spare room:

> **Theatres:** If you have a local theatre in your area, reach out to them to get on their preferred accommodation list. Actors come from all over the country (and sometimes world) and will often needs digs, especially if in a touring production.

> **Sports clubs:** Professional or amateur, sports clubs often have people travelling from area to area in need of accommodation.

> **Local businesses:** Many companies often have staff or visitors from out of town that could benefit from a

spare room in the local area.

> **Conference and wedding venues:** Often, these places don't have enough accommodation for all visitors, so it's worth getting on their radar to let them know what you can offer.

> **Places of worship:** These can attract guests and visitors from out of town who need accommodation.

> **Social clubs and societies:** Organisations like the National Trust receive a massive rental income from their properties, so there is clearly a market. If you live near a popular National Trust or English Heritage site this will bring people to the area you live in, some of whom will be looking for accommodation.

When you are ready to meet with these companies, always be polite and tailor your pitch to the environment you are in. For example, if you meet a sports club representative have some knowledge about them and their team so you can slip nuggets of information into the conversation which shows them that you care. Ultimately, you need to reassure them that if they use your services, their employees or guests will be in safe and capable hands.

Before getting in touch with organisations, think about your approach, what makes you unique and how to network with them. As the old saying goes, 'people buy off people that they like', and that exact notion is applicable for renting. You must show these organisations that you have something they need, and be approachable and professional at all times – remember, the people you network with won't only use your services but, if done correctly, will also refer you to others.

Think about branding. Simple tricks like naming your room can help you stand out from the crowd and make you appear more personable/attractive to potential renters. Depending on your offering and target demographic, things like 'The Loft', 'The Nest' or 'The Green Suite', followed by your geographical area, give your room an identity that will intrigue potential clients.

You will also want to build a website or, at the minimum, a social media page. This is all about visibility and creating a way for you and any potential organisations you are working with to share your offering as far and wide as possible. There are so many free website building tools available that this doesn't need to be a costly exercise.

Create some literature that sells your rental offering – this doesn't need to be an expensive brochure (you are a small business), but it should be attractive to potential clients. Something as simple as an A4 sheet, which has the accommodation information, some pictures and pricing. It can help to also include the location and its proximity to transport links, restaurants and stadiums. Ensure this document has an email and telephone number for any enquiries, and, if cost effective, laminate your documents for longevity.

My last trick, if you have a little cash to help with marketing, is to greet potential clients with a gift. This is a simple and effective way to keep your business offering in someone's thoughts. There are the obvious gifts like branded pens and mugs, but I often find something like a small plant with a branded pot is more unique and attractive. With a plant, or even some seeds, in a branded pot, you will be giving potential clients something they have to nurture and care for, and which they will look at daily – ensuring you and your rental room(s) are always at the forefront of their mind.

Finally, offer a discount for them and their visitors/guests if they sign up to use you there and then. Discounts work on the basis of urgency, so by offering them one within the meeting you are giving them the opportunity to save money – the anticipation of missing out if they don't sign up will give you a better chance of securing business.

Before you leave, make sure that you schedule a follow up call or meeting in the future.

Rent out your spare room(s) and other areas in your home for other purposes

Don't want to rent out your home to humans? Then renting out rooms for storage is a perfect way to earn some extra cash from your unused space. Did you know, renting out space for storage could earn you up to £1,250 a month? This is a perfect example of 'passive income' – money made without having to do anything.

There are of course, massive corporate companies who provide storage solutions to millions of people, so I advise you to market your space(s) at 50 per cent less than their rates. This makes you the more attractive alternative and if you're in a rural area, you can really benefit from the big multinational firms not having a presence.

By renting out your spare space(s), you are in complete control of the process – you can decide to operate a drop-off and pick-up service only, or offer specific times and dates items can be viewed or picked up. I would always offer spare spaces that have private access so that renting this space doesn't impact your personal or professional life – spaces like garages, basements, sheds and granny annex – if the space you rent has private access you can even provide the renter with a key, so that you don't have to be involved at all. However, if access to such space is via your private property, make sure that you set parameters for when this is allowed.

Funnily enough, garages are one of the main untapped sources of income. According to research conducted by RAC insurance, half of the country's garages (a mammoth 5.7 million) are currently not used. That's likely to be a jaw-dropping billion pounds' worth of revenue not being realised each year! If you charge £1 per square foot of your garage, you could earn around £156 per month, which would boost your annual income by £1,872 – excuse me whilst I pick my jaw up!

There are loads of other rooms you can rent out for storage and I have highlighted a few along with the average revenue from each here:

> **Spare rooms:** They're not usually privately accessible but on average, you can rent them out for storage at 80 pence per square foot, earning you on average £90 per month.

> **Lofts:** This space appears to be the most lucrative and can rent out for £2.70 per square foot. On average this could equal a rental revenue of £900 per month!

> **Basements:** The going rate for this space is £1 per square foot so on average could earn you £190 per calendar month.

As the storage space rental market continues to boom, multiple companies are setting up platforms within this area to help connect communities with a sustainable way to help each other out. Those like Stashbee, which connects people with spare space to those who need it. You get the benefit of being on a pretty big platform which can find you renters for your space much quicker.

There are commission fees and various T&Cs, so always read the small print, but if you want your spare space to start working for you quickly, pairing up with a platform could help – and remember, making 80 per cent of what your space could earn you is better than the 0 per cent your current spare space is bringing you.

The last space I want to discuss with you is car parking spaces! Most certainly within cities and large towns, parking comes at a premium and many of you have car parking spaces lying empty and dormant. In fact, there are millions of parking spaces and driveways unused across the nation which could be earning you thousands of pounds a year. This is an easy way to line your pockets with very little effort. My latest research suggests that you could earn, on average, £200 per calendar month. This can be raised significantly if you live near high demand locations such as:

> Train stations

> Sports stadiums

> Shopping centres

> Business parks

> City and town centres

A great way to start this process and to understand what your car parking space could earn you is by visiting www.parklet.co.uk – you can put in your postcode and see similar spaces around you and what they are charging. One thing to check is if you have a parking permit, as many of these carry restrictions with regards to renting your space.

If you can rent your parking space, the control is once again in your hands, so you can opt for hourly rental, daily, weekly or even longer.

A simple internet search will show you multiple sites that you can use to promote and source bookings for your parking space. Many of them are free so you can increase your chances by listing it in multiple places. Whilst they are free to advertise on, you do get charged a fee when a booking is confirmed, so shop around and find a fee you're happy with. Not to be a size queen but the bigger the platform, the more likely your space will be rented for the entire time you want it to be – bigger market presence, equals more likelihood of successes.

Here are a few to get your started but shop around and find the best platform for you:

Parklet

This is a well-established site that tends to offer longer-term rentals for people looking to rent a parking space for a month or above. You might think they are on the expensive end of the scale but they do work for their money by dealing with the contracts, processing all payments and listings are free.

You'll see here why they are best used for longer term rentals, as the fees are 30 per cent commission +VAT on daily bookings; 25 per cent +VAT on weekly bookings; 20 per cent +VAT on monthly bookings – plus a one-off £25 admin fee.

Justpark

This is a well-known platform with good feedback from parking suppliers and users. Listing is free and this platform handles all contracts and processes payments. You can rent your space out on a daily weekly or monthly basis. They only charge a 3 per cent commission fee so they land a golden star sticker from me!

Your Parking Space

This is your cheapest option because they don't charge you, the supplier, they charge the end user – which, in normal folk talk, is the person renting the space. This platform charges the 'end user' a 20 per cent commission on top of what you are advertising the space for – so do your maths homework and make sure that the final end price to the renter isn't greater than other spots up for rent in your area.

As I said, these are just three of the MANY parking rental platforms that can help you secure regular bookings for your space, but you will also need to do your homework. As I mentioned earlier, if you have a permit for your space, you need to check the T&Cs that it isn't assigned to a reg plate and therefore cannot be used by others. You will also need to check that there is nothing in your insurance which prohibits you from renting this space, nor in your mortgage or tenancy agreement, and always look into what any additional revenue might do to your income tax.

Lastly, I have heard of some overzealous councils asking for planning application fees by arguing that renting is a 'change of use' to your parking space, but the government has said it is fine as long as it isn't causing a nuisance to your neighbours. So, as with everything in life, think of those around you and make sure you're making extra cash without disturbing those within your community.

In summary...

As you will have discovered, you can pretty much rent out anything that you own. We've talked about some of the more popular things that you can rent, but the opportunity is endless.

So, before we move on, here are my must dos and don'ts to have a healthy and successful rental income.

> Do pros and cons for the platforms you want to use – ensure they meet your needs with regards to insurance levels, renter vetting schemes and commission rates.

> Read the small print – I cannot stress this enough. Please do not presume things: read the terms and conditions before you embark on renting anything.

> If you are renting anything that may store private, personal information, wipe it first. So if you are renting your laptop, only ever save your files on a separate, removable drive, never to the desktop or hard drive.

> Understand the time it takes to rent various items and keep a clear and up-to-date calendar so that you don't double book.

> Only rent good quality items – the time you have to invest will not be worth it if the item is in a bad condition.

> Be competitive with your rates – I call this the Gold-ilocks approach. You want your item to hit the sweet spot: too high and you'll alienate people, too low you might cause suspicion on the quality of your item.

> Pictures say a thousand words – so make sure you take quality images that best reflect what you are renting. Aim for a 4:3 ratio and most camera phones these days will capture 12 megapixels.

> Cash is king but a close second is information – give as much of an accurate description and detail as possible when listing your items.

> Market yourself, too. Fat Llama found that people who upload a picture of themselves and a short biography to their profile see 60 per cent more rental action than those who don't. Remember the saying 'people buy from people that they like'? Well, I'm adapting it to 'people rent from people they feel they know'.

> Be responsive. In a world where information is instant, renters will expect answers to questions quickly otherwise they will move on.

> Finally, be courteous, helpful and polite. It should go without saying generally in life, but if people like you, they will re-use your services and recommend you to others.

Renting out your stuff is all about being entrepreneurial – look at the items and space around you that you could turn from dust collectors to money makers! Renting your items can be fun and, most importantly, it can bring in much needed additional income. So now is the time for you to give it a go – I've given you loads of information, ideas, dos and don'ts, but the rest is up to you.

Take a look at the template table below and use it to create your very own rental stocklist. Fill in the items you would be happy to rent out and you'll soon see how much money they can be making you per month!

Item	Average £ per day/week	Target rental days per month	Total revenue for month

We've established that you can rent out most of the things in your life, so if you are new to this, I suggest starting small and expanding when you understand the time and effort it takes for the various different categories. GOOD LUCK!

TIPS FROM YOUR TECH

I'm guilty of it, my husband is most definitely guilty of it and so I think it would be fair of me to assume that you are guilty of it too.

As a nation, we have between £16 and £20 billion worth of unused technology. Which means that each of us, on average, is sitting on about £800 worth of tech that we do not use but could make us money. It's estimated that each of us has 11 or more tech items which we could easily sell for some decent cash.

I could hardly believe the statistics, so I rummaged around my home to see what my husband has and I was amazed to find not one but three old phones, an old laptop, two old computer consoles with various additions and games, plus a small TV he must have had since before we met. This was all from just a quick search through his storage, so I am sure there is much more I will find and transform into money for the future.

Technology develops at a rapid pace, which fuels consumerism and ultimately leads to a surplus in the tech items in our homes. Whether its laptops or digital cameras, not only do they take up space but they could, more importantly, be making you a pretty hefty profit. In 2021, the second-hand electronics market was estimated to be worth a staggering, £4.75 billion in the UK and will, I am sure, continue to grow annually.

Whilst the wealthy drive demand for brand new, many of us, either conscious of the environment and trying to mitigate damage to the planet, or merely due to budget, are turning to second-hand technology. Have you heard of Laver's Law – the speed at which fashion does a full 360: in fashion, out and then back in? Well, apply the same principle to technology and this explains why so many people have a genuine nostalgia for old tech.

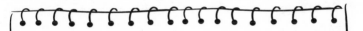

Dan's Top Tip

Sell your old tech as soon as you stop using it to make more money. Whilst there is some vintage technology out there which sells for big bucks, most of what we have will start to depreciate in the short-to-medium term, so the quicker you flog it, the sooner you'll have extra money in your pocket.

Please don't forget that before you try to sell any of your old tech, you need to make sure that you have wiped any personal information from the device and returned it to factory settings. The process is easy to perform and there will be clear instructions to follow in your item's manual. If, like me, you have already misplaced or thrown away the manual, the internet is a great resource for online versions.

Or you can always go to a relevant manufacturer or retail outlet for guidance. Cyber fraud is prolific so I can't stress enough how important it is to do this before you start selling.

Below I have categorised a broad range of technology items that you might see lying around your home and I've highlighted the gems which can make you serious cash, but the list isn't extensive – gosh, I'd need to write an entire book solely on selling tech if I was to capture everything. As you know, I harp on about doing your research, and some of the websites I mention later in the chapter will give you an idea of the value of your tech item if I don't cover it here.

Phones

It's probably no surprise that mobile phones are the most obvious spare tech you have in your possession. Remember, I found three of my husband's! Well, he isn't alone; 81 per cent of us have one, if not more, old mobile phone that we no longer use. According to research from Giffgaff, there are an estimated 55 million mobile phones in perfectly good condition that could be sold.[7]

Some of the more unique and first edition phones can earn you a whopping £1,000, but generally, for this sort of price tag, you'd need something like the Motorola DynaTAC 8000X, which was the first commercially available mobile phone from 1983. One of these sold a few years ago for £1,776 and it's not the only mobile to demand such a high price tag – an unopened, first edition iPhone once sold on eBay for $190,372.80. Now, I doubt many of us have one of these just gathering dust in a box, but you'd be surprised how much their successors go for. Whilst first editions can be extremely lucrative, mid-to-late 1980s phones also demand a decent price tag.

10 valuable second-hand mobile phones are:

1. Motorola DynaTAC 8000X, £1,000–£2,000

2. Nokia Mobira Senator, up to £3,000 in good condition

3. IBM Simon Personal Communicator, £1,500–£4,000

4. 2011 BlackBerry Porsche, up to £2,000

5. The first iPhone model known as the iPhone 2G, up to £1,000.

6. The slider-style Nokia 8810, thousands in great condition but even if not, around £500

7. 1989 Ericsson GH 198, up to £1,500 depending on its condition

8. Nokia 9000 Communicator – one of the earliest smartphones on the market, released in 1996 – £800 in good condition

9. 2009 Sony Ericsson W995, £500

10. Motorola Star TAC, in decent condition, £400

As I mentioned earlier, even if you don't have one of these big price tag mobile phones, all of them retain a value, so whether that's £20 or £200, surely it's worth a little elbow grease to line your pockets? Some of the more common models include:

> Nokia 3310, up to £300

> BlackBerry 957, up to £250

> Sony Ericsson w800i, £80

> LG Chocolate, £50

> Nokia 8210, £20

> Motorola Razr V3, £50

> Samsung SGH-E250, £20

> Sony Ericsson k800i, £30

> Nokia 7110, £70

> BlackBerry Curve 8520, £40

> Nokia 5110, £50

According to the World Economic Forum, there are now more mobile phones in the world than people and it is estimated that by 2025 there will be over 18 billion mobile devices operating in the world. So even if you don't have one of the ones I have highlighted, such is the demand; it's likely that it will still make you some cash.

TVs

I am pretty confident that many of us will have an unused TV in our home and whilst I don't have any hard facts or data on how many spares we have in the UK, I am sure it is a lot. There are various reasons why I am so confident that many of you will have a television you could sell. One of the most obvious is children flying the nest but parents keeping their room as it was for whenever they might return. Another is that as a society, we are changing the way we consume media. Many of us, and especially the younger generation, are watching media on laptops, mobile phones and other devices, placing less demand on the television in your home. Bensons For Beds did some research and estimate that 17 per cent of all media is now viewed on devices other than televisions, and I have no doubt that this number will rise.[8] So, with our changing viewing habits and the free-flowing of family members in and out of our homes, don't overlook this money-making resource.

I also want to discuss TVs in the bedroom. Further research from Bensons For Beds concluded that 57 per cent of us have a TV in the bedroom and I want to encourage you all to get out of this habit for two reasons: health and wealth.[9]

Various studies have documented that watching TV in your bedroom can stop you sleeping, cause you to have less sleep and mean you get less quality sleep once you do eventually nod off. I am a terrible sleeper so if there is anything I would be prepared to lose to gain more, I would.

Unlike with other technology, I haven't seen signs of any nostalgic trend in televisions, so a general rule of thumb is that the older they are, the less you will make from them. If the make and model of your TV is still for sale, I'd advise you to price up your second-hand one at about 50–60 per cent of its current retail price as new. With new TV models coming out so regularly, it wouldn't make sense for me to list some of the generics as they'd be out of date before this book is even published, but take a look at the various websites I mention later and you will get a decent idea of the value your old TV could hold.

That said, some much older TV sets can be worth several hundred pounds, so keep an eye out if you have any of the following:

> Bush TV22, produced in the 1950s

> Ferguson 3453, a 1960s portable black and white TV

> Ferguson 3753, produced in the 1970s

> Murphy A122, from the 1950s

> Pye V4, 1960s. Collectors go mad for its retro style

Computers

Next up, we have computers. For ease, when I talk about computers in this section, I have grouped them to include laptops, desktops and tablets.

Computers are something that all of us own, yet it is surprising how little we use them. You might remember in the previous chapter, the staggering fact is that whilst 61 per cent of the population own a computer, 42 per cent of us claim to hardly use it.

As the technological revolution shows no signs of slowing down, some people will find that they have excess computers just because they have bought new to keep up with the latest designs and software. Also, many households have multiple computers which could easily be condensed into one that is shared. One family of four who are my friends, have 12 devices in their home, as each has their own desktop, laptop and tablet. Obviously, if you can truly justify this and you do need all of them due to work, school and other reasons, that's up to you, but if you want a quick and easy way to make some cash, this could be it. When I challenged the aforementioned family about how often they used each device and how necessary it was on a regular basis, they realised they could downsize this tech to four devices. So they have eight devices that, I worked out, could sell for roughly £2,000, and which are hardly used.

As with TVs, generally these devices are worth more the newer they are; however, there are some gems from years ago that are worth keeping your eyes out for:

> The first personal computer to come with a warranty was the Apple-1. These are so rare and sought after that in recent auctions they have gone for anything from £250,000 to £1 million.

> The first personal computer created by IBM was the IBM 5150. Depending on its condition and configuration, these can sell for anything from a few hundred to a few thousand pounds.

> Launched in 1975, the IBM 5100 portable computer can sell from £3,500 to £8,000.

> Released in 1977, the Commodore PET 2001, depending on its condition, can sell from several hundred pounds up to a thousand.

> Vintage collectors still go giddy for the Amiga 1000, released by Commodore in 1985. You can expect to sell these for north of £500.

> A Microsoft Tablet PC, which was launched in 2002, can raise £150 to £350.

> The Apple PowerBook 100 first came onto the scene in 1991. In good condition, this early Apple laptop can raise £350 to £720.

Another great source of cash is games consoles. Sold with games, they can really generate much needed additional funds but always research your games before selling them, as some games hold a higher value and you don't want to lose out by bundling those with the console. I'm sure it goes without saying that the higher earning consoles are the biggest names, like Nintendo, PlayStation and Xbox.

It's likely that many families will have the odd games console stored away somewhere, due to the fact that years ago, we were less well-informed about re-selling and sustainability, so just put these items to the back of the cupboard when we stopped playing with them.

Some of the most popular consoles you may have are:

> The classic 1980s Nintendo Entertainment System (NES). This was the original mass-produced games console and, as such, can sell from £50 to £200, depending on the condition, but there are some very rare games that can go for a fortune. There were only 116 cartridges of the Nintendo World Championships 1990 ever made so they are worth hundreds of thousands of pounds, and the Nintendo Campus Challenge game is worth tens of thousands of pounds.

> Super Nintendo (SNES) released in the 1990s sells for a similar price to its predecessor at £50 to £200

> Sega Mega Drive will fetch you £40 to £150

> Sega Saturn can sell for £50 to £150

> Sony PlayStation, £50 to £300

> Sega Dreamcast, £50 to £150

> Sega Game Gear, £150 to £350

> Atari 2600 sells anywhere from £100 upwards but, like the NES, some of the games for this console can seriously push up the asking price. The most jaw-dropping is the game Air Raid, which could be worth over £26,000.

When it comes to vintage consoles, Gameboys can be extremely lucrative. When I researched the price increase of Gameboys since their inception, I was shocked to work out that, on average, they have increased in value by 191.7 per cent. There are very few items in the world that are seeing such a high percentage rise in value. As with most mass-produced consoles, there are various editions and models, so only a few demand the biggest price tags.

> Gameboy Light, released in Japan, £200 to £400

> Pokémon edition, £150 to £300

> Gameboy Advance, £200 to £300

These lists are a selection of some of my favourites, by way of illustration of the sorts of prices they fetch. If you have a different console, some simple research can inform you of the price you should sell it on for.

Other tech

Some other tech items you may not use or need that you could consider selling include:

> Smart speakers

> Washing machines and dryers

> Vacuum cleaners

> Home audio systems: CD players, tape players, stereos

> Printers and scanners

> Fitness trackers and smart watches

> Kitchen appliances (fridges, microwaves, air fryers, pasta makers, slow cookers)

> Digital photo frames

> eBook readers

> Drones

> DVD players

As I mentioned, it would be a rather big task to identify and highlight every single piece of tech you can sell, but my headline advice is to look around your home, look at what technology you barely use and do some research about its value – when you see those pound signs, it will most likely motivate you to get rid of it.

Due to the value of the second-hand tech market, there are loads of outlets where you can sell your unused or unwanted technology. The best place may often depend on the item, whether you want to go broad with mass appeal or whether you need to find the specialist collectors who are on the lookout for unusual and rare items.

The first thing I want you to do is complete the template below and list all the tech you want to sell.

Item	1st valuation	2nd valuation	3rd valuation	RRP (add all valuations and divide by three)
1)				
2)				
3)				
4)				
5)				

Now you need to go and find three valuations for each so that we can work out your recommended retail price (RRP). According to the company Compare and Recycle, the average person loses £87 when selling an old mobile phone because they settle for the first price offered rather than doing the research and shopping around.

Here are some of the sites I suggest using to get valuations for the items you want to sell:

> www.musicmagpie.co.uk

> www.zapper.co.uk

> www.comparemymobile.com

> www.envirofone.com

> www.webuyanyphone.com

> www.spring.co.uk

Once you have secured three valuations for every item you want to sell, you can add them up, divide them by three and then you'll have the RRP, which is the lowest amount you should be selling the item for..

The sites mentioned above are good places where you may want to sell your unwanted tech but remember to shop around and look at all costs associated with various platforms to ensure you are putting the most money in your own pocket.

Dan's Top Tip

The less you have to do, the less you will make. All these sites offer a service that can earn you cash for your old tech very quickly, but shop around as so many variables affect the offer you will get.

If you have the spare time and you want to maximise the money you could make, you could look at doing the heavy lifting yourself to make more. Online marketplaces where you cut out the middle person means you can earn more money, but you will have to do the work to get the item sold and sent. Facebook Marketplace and eBay are the most common and trusted. Set yourself up with an account, take clear pictures of your tech and write detailed descriptions. Remember, buyers don't want to do the work, so if you put in the extra effort you'll be more likely to sell it quickly.

Another option is www.ecoatm.com, who assure users that the devices you sell to them will be recycled or reused, therefore ensuring a more sustainable method helping to reduce electronic waste whilst still earning your fair profit from it. At the time of publication, this company has ecoATMs – hole-in-the-wall, cash machine-looking kiosks – dotted around 53 UK cities. You simply place your device in one of the machines, it analyses the item and offers you a price that you can either accept or decline.

Some well-known suppliers will also offer you cash or vouchers to trade in your old tech, but always read the small print as often trade-ins are only used towards you purchasing something new in the specific retail outlet.

Places you can try include:

> Currys

> Carphone warehouse

> Apple

> Argos

> EE

> Amazon – which is a particularly great trade-in partner, as they take everything from your smart speaker to your ring doorbells and streaming devices; in fact, most technology is allowed here

Social media platforms are a great way to tap into enthusiasts and collectors. In my experience, and as a rather keen collector myself, most of us belong to groups on social media where we help each other find items we are looking to complete our sets or help others to sell them. If you sell via this method, there will rarely be a fee associated with selling direct. Pop the keyword into a search engine and it will likely yield you a group or forum via which you can sell any of your tech.

Last but by no means least, there are always high street shops like Pawnbrokers and companies like CEX. They will buy certain items of your old tech, but the price they offer may be lower than online sites because these stores have overheads and operating costs. The benefit to these locations is that they can do a deal there and then if you are in need of some additional funds instantly.

The average person spends £943.40 on their annual holiday and we are each sat on roughly £800 worth of unwanted tech. So just think what a boost this could be as you plan the next family trip together.

WARDROBE WAGES

Of all the things in your home that could make you instant cash, clothing is the most accessible, the easiest to sort and quite often the least missed. I normally dislike repeating myself, but I think that it's important to do so in this instance because the facts are so shocking. As I mentioned in Chapter 6, it is estimated that we have around £30 billion in unwanted clothing lying around the UK in our homes and we fill landfills with around 350,000 tonnes of clothing per year.

A lot of this excess fashion in our wardrobes comes from the fast fashion, and how easy and cheap it is for us to purchase an outfit that we may never wear. Online shopping has also made it so simple to purchase but quite often a lot of us don't want the hassle of returning the items. One major online auction site found that 65 per cent of clothes purchased need to be returned, but they languish in our homes because we don't read the returns policy in time or simply forget. We are all guilty of it; I ordered some beach-wear that didn't fit once, went on holiday and then forgot about it.

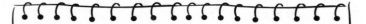

Dan's Top Tip

Always purchase items ahead of when you intend to wear them and leave the tags on for 3–4 days. I call this my cooling-off period: a couple of days to think about whether I like the item, will wear it and utilise it. If not, you can return it by following the specific returns policy. Pop a note on a calendar to remind you if you're like me and likely to forget about it.

Sorting through your clothes to decide what to keep and what to sell will not only do great things for your pocket but will also help the environment. If as a society we re-purposed or re-used other people's fashion, we could collectively drive down the need for new production and the carbon footprint of the clothing market.

Before you sell any of your clothes, complete my simple four steps to get you sale ready:

1. Familiarise yourself with your fashion

Let's be honest, how many of us know every item of clothing we have? So, get familiar with your wardrobe. Pull out all the clothes you own and lay them out to look at. I need you to properly scrutinise each piece of clothing and ask yourself whether you wear it often or hardly ever. I find looking at my phone or social media quite a good research tool to identify what I do and do not wear. Be strict: a pretty top hanging unused in your wardrobe isn't doing anything to help your cashflow.

2. Condition is king

You need to inspect all your clothes and the condition they are in. Any holes, stretched material, loss of original colour or faded patterns will not sell well. The truth is that some items do get worn to the point where you don't want to wear them, but these items can be put to good use at a clothes bank. Clothes banks will accept worn or ripped goods because if they can't re-sell an item it can be reused and recycled. So, whilst they are not making you money they, will be put to good use and avoid adding to the land-fill problem. Remember, if you try to pull the wool over a buyer's eyes by selling something tatty, it will be returned and you'll have to cover the cost to sort this, also wasting your time and efforts.

3. Don't get personal

As lovely as your undergarments are they've touched parts of you that shouldn't be shared . . . I think there are sites for that but not ones in my arsenal. I digress. Keep your used socks, bras, knickers, and anything that has touched your personal delicates, off the sales list.

4. Don't be the next editor of *Vogue*

You may think you have a keen eye for fashion but don't let your personal taste cloud your judgement. Your taste is not universal and as we know with Laver's Law (more on this below), fashions trends follow a cycle and are returning quicker than ever before. I would bet my own hard cash on the fact that hundreds of thousands of those clothes lying in landfill have been put there because someone thought they were out of fashion. Just because you don't like it anymore doesn't mean others won't pay a decent amount for it.

In addition to Laver's Law, some items in your wardrobe may be deemed vintage and in high demand so can carry a higher price tag. Clothes can sometimes be like wine – they can get better with age. Laver's Law chronologically maps the lifespan of fashion trends. This covers the time from when it was released, when it became a fashion must-have, then a fashion no-no, before finally turning full circle and coming back into fashion. Originally this period was 150 years for a style of clothing to first hit the market and then return but we are seeing fashion trends return within 30 years nowadays.

Fashion is cyclical, so if your clothes are in good condition, the price you can ask for them may actually go up. In fashion today, we can see a huge demand for clothes from the 1990s. As the world slowly became a smaller place in the 1990s due to the rise of the internet and mobile phones, cultures and different socioeconomic communities began influencing each other far more than had previously been possible, thus creating some bold, eclectic and experimental fashion.

We witnessed sports and leisure wear entering the mainstream as a result of the hip hop influence, plaid shirts and oversized clothing was made popular by grunge culture, and later Britney Spears and the Spice Girls resulted in a rise of pastels and feminine tones in clothing.

With buyers chasing these 'vintage' (I hate that my teenage years can be referred to as 'vintage'!) styles, I have seen plenty items going for decent cash. Things like:

> Chanel sunglasses for £300

> Football shirts rising up to £100

> North Face puffer jackets reaching £100

I personally think this is because current designers are taking inspiration from their youth and parents. So influential stars such as Justin Bieber and Kim Kardashian wearing contemporary items that have been influenced by an era drive the demand for these old clothes, whilst other people's desire to be more sustainable and renounce fast fashion also makes vintage a money-making opportunity.

Nostalgia is a strong driving force for this market and, whilst I don't usually claim to be able to tell the future, I can confidently predict that the clothes you are wearing today will become collectable in a few decades.

So definitely pay attention to any old clothes that may fall into the vintage bracket; you could even hold back some select clothes that may only be 10–15 years old and wait for them to hit the sweet spot in about 10 years' time.

One thing I often tell people to be mindful of is the seasons. Look at how you buy and when, plus what all the retail outlets try to do. Rarely will you find big winter coats on sale in the summer, just as you're unlikely to see a shop trying to sell swimming trunks in the winter. Occasionally, because of foreign travel people may need an item out of season, but I want you to appeal to the mass market to sell as much of your unwanted fashion as possible. Compliment the time of year to cash in.

I find it really useful to sell clothes by categories. It helps me to be targeted and clearly showcases what items of clothes you will be able to purchase from me. This can also influence where you sell.

Below are some of the categories I often sell my unwanted clothes in:

> Sports items

> Formal wear

> 1990s clothing

> High street

> High end

Every chapter of my book is designed to help you realise the cash in your own bubble and a reoccurring theme is to know your pricing strategy. Price yourself too high and people might think you are trying to rip them off – even if you would be prepared to lower your price, you've probably lost that customer before the conversation. Price yourself too low and people will question the quality. First impressions count and you rarely get a chance to make a second one, so that's why your pricing is key.

There are a few ways you can work out your price point for each item. I always suggest keeping an eye on what your item would retail for new, especially designer goods if you are lucky enough to have them. Research the market – can you see similar second-hand goods for sale and if so, at what price point? Whilst there isn't an internationally agreed formula for pricing your old clothes, I generally go with the rule of 20–40 per cent of the original price, depending on age and condition.

> 40 per cent is the top end for relatively new items.

> 30 per cent is for items that are a few years old.

> 20 per cent is for anything 10–20 years old.

Anything that has hit the sweet spot of being in its vintage years should be heavily researched to work out supply and demand and therefore your price point.

In addition to this, anything that has original packaging and price tags can demand a much higher asking price if you can prove it hasn't been worn. And please don't forget to work out your packaging and posting costs (P&P); these should always be thought through and considered within your pricing strategy. Don't try to make a profit in this area – use your actual hard costs of what it will cost to package up and post the item. If you're an online seller, the likelihood is that your buyers are experienced, so they'll know the deals they can get elsewhere for postage and packaging. Trying to outsmart your buyers for a couple of extra quid profit isn't going to do you any good.

For certain items you might want to offer free P&P to entice buyers. I would often suggest this for luxury, high-worth items to offer a gesture of goodwill when they are parting with larger sums of money.

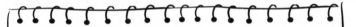

Dan's Top Tip

Don't set your pricing strategy in stone. Everyone loves a bargain so being able to offer small discounts can help you to seal more deals. The trick is to price your items at fair and market competitive cost but leave yourself some wiggle room in order to be able to barter with buyers who are sticklers for a good deal.

Once you've sorted your pricing strategy, you need to get your items ready to sell. I hope this goes without saying but it is vital that you have washed/cleaned the items and ironed them where necessary. Obviously, follow the manufacturer's care instructions when you do this. This isn't just to ensure a buyer receives them clean, but also so they look good in the pictures you'll take of the items to help sell them. If you can't remember my tips and tricks of how to best photograph your items, head back to Chapter 6 where I give you a beginner's guide to the best photography to showcase your items.

When writing descriptions of your items, always include the name of the brand and the size of the item. Don't use generic sizing – be specific with exact measurements of the waist, inside leg, shoulder length, as over the years, what was classified as a 'medium' or a female 14, may have changed. Include details of the material it's made from and any faults. I know we discussed not selling items that are torn or have holes, but items with a missing strap or button might still attract a sale to an upcycler.

Where to sell
Where to sell your clothes will depend on your offering, but if you want to make a decent profit for less leg work, using online sites might be the quickest option.

As the online selling world continues to grow, more and more sites are becoming bespoke whilst some of the big global organisations stay broad. There are far too many sites to discuss them all so I have highlighted some of my favourite, most trusted sites to give you a steer.

Best for premium goods
I would suggest using Vestiaire Collective, which is a top choice for selling items that you want a premium for. If you want to be earning over £60 an item, this site will put you in good company and people come here knowing they are

going to be spending more for the items they really want. I admit, I have seen items on this site selling for as low as £14, but generally they are more expensive. Be honest with yourself and be confident anything you list here is capable of achieving premium price tags. Don't be delusional and think that just because you listed something on a higher end site, that it will reach a higher premium. This won't work if it's your basic level fast fashion you bought for pennies.

As with many online sites, this platform will take a fee for listing your items. At the time of writing all items priced between £80 to £13,000 have a selling fee of 15 per cent and a 3 per cent processing fee. Any items under £80 have a fixed fee of £12 per item and for anything over £13,000 there is a fixed fee of £2,000.

I appreciate that some people don't want to pay fees, but always look at what benefits using a prestigious site can bring. They have a loyal client base, are trusted and tap into the type of clothes you are wanting to sell, and they take care of most of the practicalities. Once a sale is agreed, you basically post the item to the company who check the item is what you have advertised and then they process it and get it to the buyer. This really helps if you are time poor and you will still be earning roughly, on average, 75 per cent of the price you market the item at. Once Vestiaire is happy with your item, they transfer the money the next day, so the cash can start to add up as quickly as you can sell.

Marketplaces are best for no fees, but you do all the legwork
Shpock and Facebook Marketplace are two of the best known, but there are loads. These sites operate on a no charge basis, so you keep 100 per cent of the sale price you agree. As long as you market within your local area, there

won't be any additional postage and packaging cost; you can hand deliver the item or advertise for collection only. Most of these sites are easy to use and straightforward to understand.

Being a huge car boot fan myself, local community selling sites to me are like the car boots of the digital era. So be prepared to put the art of bartering you learned in Chapter 4 to the test as a lot of your customers will be serious bargain hunters.

There is no hard rule on what you can and cannot sell on these sites but I find that the lower value items will shift quicker than more specialist or expensive. Things like second-hand children's clothes do particularly well.

Best for volume and broad appeal

eBay will deliver you quick sales on all sorts of clothing due to the sheer number of customers using this platform. Due to it being so broad, you will be able to advertise all sorts of clothes on here because there is probably a buyer on the other side of a computer screen.

Dan's Top Tip

I must warn you, though, digital scamming is rife and this includes people trying to purchase items on community-based sites. So always make sure you receive full payment, cleared into your account before you send any of your clothes. If you are meeting in person, do so in a public space with lots of people around, take a friend if possible and ask for cash before handing anything over.

But be realistic with your pricing. Like Vestiaire, eBay also charges fees, which, at the time of writing is 12.8 per cent of the final sale price plus a 30 pence transaction fee. eBay often holds great incentives to engage sellers so keep an eye out for their offerings and how this may help you get rid of a load of unused clothes for an easily earned profit.

Best site for the cool kids

Depop has a vast youth appeal and whilst I am sure oldies like myself are welcome to shop there, they do say that 90 per cent of their users are under 26 years old and 1 in 3 of their users are 15–24 year olds with an account on their app. You're not charged a listing fee and the commission for any sold items is a respectable 10 per cent, so it really is an easy-to-use platform, tapped into a specific demographic that will benefit you if you have the items these clients are after.

Remember, if you are closer to my age than the site's under-26 demographic, the likelihood is that you have some 1980s, '90s and '00s fashion items that they'll bite your arm off for.

The best all-rounder

Vinted is the platform where you can find all sorts of clothing and it has mass appeal to a broad demographic of people, styles and fashions. It's simple to navigate and use and they don't charge the seller a price to list or any fees on your final sale price. How they make their money is by charging the buyer a buyer's protection fee. So always remember to add this percentage in your pricing strategy to see if your item will be able to secure that overall price tag. That fee varies from 3–8 per cent and they charge a transaction fee to the buyer of between 30–80p per item.

As mentioned, these are just a couple of my suggestions for you to explore. There are many others, like Etsy and Preloved, so dig deep and do your research for the best sites for your clothes.

Once you have found your perfect platform, make sure you share that you are selling on it. Regardless of your following, promote that you are selling your clothes across your social media platforms and get friends and family to share the message too. The more your advertisement is shared, the more likely it will land in the laptop of someone who wants to buy your goods.

The final thing you need to learn about selling is that your reputation precedes you. This goes for everything *Money Maker* teaches you but is crucial within the online selling world. Becoming a bubble entrepreneur means that your business is yourself, so you need to grow and develop a solid reputation for being fair, honest and easy to buy from. The digital landscape offers people an instant way to discredit and complain about you, so don't give them this opportunity; instead, make sure that they want to leave positive and supportive reviews about what a pleasure you are to deal with.

A couple of my headline tips on becoming a successful salesperson are:

> Always be polite when answering questions or queries and try to be as quick as possible when replying.

> Be honest, up front and always do your best to manage expectations.

> Put a little thank you note in with the item when you

send it asking for a review and offer a discount on any future purchases for doing so.

> Deal with complaints and concerns after the sale as promptly and politely as possible. Poor customer service at this point could mean a return and a refund, the loss of a customer for good and a poor review. Issues can often be resolved when dealt with head on and in a compassionate manner.

If you don't have access to or don't want to sell online, there are other ways to shift your old clobber. I often get sellers coming into my pawnbrokers with high-end, designer goods. If it's the right item for a pawnbroker, we can buy the item there and then and transfer or give you the cash on the spot, which is a quick and effective way to make a profit from your old items.

For other high-end items, some auction houses will take clothes and accessories but always check out what their fees are and research how successful they been in selling similar items to yours previously.

For mid- to low-level value items, I don't think anything can beat a car boot, but I am probably the car boot's biggest fan. They are a very quick and effective way to get rid of your unwanted wardrobe items and make some decent wages in the process.

Before we move on, I want to discuss one item from your wardrobe in particular: your wedding dress. I know we discussed how to monetise your wedding dress by renting it, but if you don't have the time or desire for this, your wedding dress could be the highest priced item in your wardrobe. It helps the environment and will also free up extra space at home, so it's a win win.

Below are my top tips for selling your wedding dress:

Sell sooner rather than later

The quicker you sell your dress, the more money you are likely to get. Designs in wedding dresses do evolve and change so selling within the first three or four years will help you to maximise your dress's money-making potential. My research suggests that you can ask for 50–60 per cent of the RRP in the case of a newer dress, and for those over four years old, you can still achieve a 30–40 per cent of the original cost. As usual, research your particular brand and style within the second-hand market to confirm a decent valuation.

Vintage Vaults

If you dress is over 20 years old, then research a little deeper because vintage dresses can often rise in value and demand a much higher price tag than you envisaged.

Get your dress cleaned.

Yes, it will cost you a few quid but if it's been stuck in your wardrobe or even attic for a while then having it looking all sparkly and new and smelling great will lead to more interest and greater customer satisfaction.

Great photos are vital

A great picture will help the customer visualise wearing this dress. It is intended for the biggest day of their life, so they have to be able to imagine the fairy tale. You should consider using your professional photos from your big day as you won't be able to take better ones yourself and clients can see the dress in action.

Be honest and upfront

As with your general wardrobe, ruined garments are unlikely to sell but ones with some little fixes could still earn you a decent wage. You wore it on a day filled with laughter, joy and dancing so the odd missing button or strap won't necessarily deter someone who loves the overall dress.

Details

Be precise with the fit, giving as much details on the sizing as possible. 'Size 12 but I found it tight on the chest' or similar means you are being as transparent as possible, so that you don't face a return.

There are so many online sites that can help you list and sell your wedding dress for some decent wages. I hope that it was the best day of your life but be realistic, when are you going to wear a wedding dress again? You could help someone find their ideal dress whilst also making a nice little wardrobe wage at the same time.

And finally...

I find that keeping a record of the items you have sold, on which site and for what price helps build you some clever market research to understand the selling marketplace so that you can tweak and evolve your sales strategy. Follow my easy-to-use template on the next page to keep a record and review it often to remind yourself of the successes and challenges you have experienced to fine-tune your selling prowess as you progress.

MONEY MAKER

Category.	
Item description.	
Platform.	
Price	
Price achieved	
Date advertised	
Date sold	
Satisfaction	

158

COLLECTIONS
FOR CASH

Nations across the globe are known to have unique characteristics and cultural traits which influence their identity, and
when it comes to the United Kingdom, one very clear aspect
of our identity is our obsession with collecting.

I think you'll be surprised to know that 83 per cent of Brits,
according to a study conducted by the Royal Mint, said that
they have collected something within their lifetime. This
figure is higher than any other country in the world and,
furthermore, 57 per cent of those surveyed confirmed that
they have an active collection at this very time. This is an
incredible figure and proves that collecting is engrained
within us and intrinsically reflective of Britain's complex
and complicated obsession with its class system.

Our obsession with collecting is perhaps rooted in
the history of the British Empire. As far back as the
sixteenth century, when we built ships capable of sailing
around the globe. Whilst doing so, explorers 'discovered
exotic lands' and their abundance of treasures and 'curious'

objects, which they would bring back to the UK.

As the British Empire's long and winding tentacles wrapped around the globe, this desire to obtain 'unfamiliar' and exciting items grew, embedding itself in our national psyche. As these items were brought back to the UK, it created the foundations of collecting among the wealthy aristocracy. Items not directly used for a functional purpose were just not within the financial reach of the average person before the nineteenth century.

The first industrial revolution in the eighteenth century saw the transition of making goods by hand to using machines, but the second industrial revolution in the nineteenth century was a phase of technological revolution whereby mass production really took off, enabling all classes to be able to start collecting.

Items commemorating prominent national celebrations, such as coronations and royal births, were mass produced in the form of affordable trinkets, which saw lower classes able to participate in the pastime of collecting, previously only accessible to the aristocracy and wealthy of this country. To collect had traditionally meant that you were doing well in life and moving up the social and economic ladder, but during this time period, collecting became a hobby past down from aristocrats, cultivated by the middle class and aspired to by the working class.

The list of what we can collect is almost endless and some categories that people collect are worthless. Collections of elastic bands or bouncy balls aren't going to open the door of money-making potential, but some categories could create a very healthy revenue stream. Generally speaking, you could sell an entire collection as a job lot but, whilst it is more time consuming, I suggest you sell parts of the collection separately, as this will likely yield a greater return for you.

In this chapter, we are going to be covering common collections you may have at home, how to understand their value and how to sell them. But don't skip this chapter if you're not a collector yourself. Some items in your home can still be extremely desirable to collectors and, who knows, you might have that rare final item that would complete a person's collection.

Capitalising on our national obsession with collecting and learning the tools to connect with collectors can be an extremely good money-making opportunity.

As we have discussed, historically we have been obsessed with collecting for hundreds of years, but understanding why we are still a nation of collectors to this day is a key learning if we want to know how we can make the most money from collections. We need to understand the motivations that are driving potential customers towards a potential purchase. When we know this, we can adapt our sales pitch accordingly to tap into whichever motivator has brought them to this potential deal. Below, I will talk you through some of the various motivators and how each affects the price you'll be able to achieve.

Dan's Top Tip

Identifying items that will sell for a profit is only half of the equation; working out how and to whom it is best to sell them is the other key component and this is super important when it comes to collectibles.

Nostalgia and sentimentality

These are two really strong buying motivators that most of us will have at some point. Whether it's a longing for the past or an attachment to an emotion or feeling, both of these motivators will often result in the buyer being ruled by their heart rather than their head. This ultimately will affect people's ability to negotiate because an emotional response has increased the value and importance of the item.

A sense of identity

If someone is an avid petrol enthusiast and collects model cars or books about the automotive industry, this likely is because they associate that collection as being part of their identity as a person. They need to collect because it reflects who they are. This doesn't always add to the value of an item in their head or mean that they will pay more to acquire it, though, because this isn't always an emotionally led motivator.

Collecting for monetary gain

There are many people who collect because they believe this to be a strong money-making hobby or activity. Someone who collects for this purpose will often want to barter with you to obtain the item you are attempting to sell. These are often the hardest collectors to do a deal with because their ultimate motivator is for their own financial gain, so they will want the item for the lowest possible price to turn a higher profit.

The thrill of the hunt

Many collectors are motivated by completing a collection or adding interesting pieces to their collection. They love the chase, the clamour to find new and exciting pieces. This motivator often sees heart and almost obsession take over from rational thought and will result in the collector often paying whatever is necessary to obtain the item you are selling.

Preserving history and cultural heritage

Many collectors feel it is their duty to source and preserve items that they deem to be historically or culturally important. Many collectors take great pride and satisfaction in this. Collectors motivated by this can often be driven by their emotions and pay a premium.

When put into practice, you may not always be able to understand a buyer's motivator, but it's imperative you know them so you can keep an eye out for them. It's often a case of knowing to pose some questions which may lead you to better understand their motivator.

Dan Fun Fact:
According to insurer Direct Line Select, Britons own around £220 billion worth of high value collectibles.[10]

So, I think it is fair to say that collecting is seeing its golden age. We know why people collect but why is the market exploding? I think the reason is quite simple. In a fast and ever-moving world that has become globalised, trends appear and disappear so quickly that many of us yearn for items that remind us of happy and carefree days. These are often items that have associations with our past and, as such, collecting them makes us feel a sense of comfort.

As I have already mentioned, there are infinite things that people may choose to collect but I want to discuss some of the best collectibles that can be worth a small fortune.

Stamps

I cannot tell you how many emails and calls I get regarding these. We often inherit stamps or collected them in our younger years and most people who contact me have no idea of their value. Assessing and valuing stamps is a complicated and difficult process. To ascertain how much a single stamp is worth, there are many factors that have to be considered – such as its age, its rarity, the country of issue and its condition. Because so many stamps have been created around the world, it is often difficult to get accurate prices without lots of time and effort going to the process of valuation.

Some considerations that can affect the value of stamps are:

> Stamps glued into a collections book will almost certainly lose a considerable amount of their value due to the fact this process damages the stamp.

> Errors can make you money. If you have any stamps that have a mistake on them then this will add to the value because it will be a rarity.

> Generally speaking, most of the more valuable stamps are pre-1960, although some later ones can be worth good money as well.

> Rarity is key. Stamps that had a limited production

164

run can be worth big money and, likewise, the older ones with few surviving examples can also yield big money.

> Age and historical significance is important too. Stamps depicting events of the past can be worth a pretty penny.

> Condition is important. Unused stamps will likely carry a premium.

Some stamps are worth a staggering amount of money. The highest value top five are:

1. 1863 Plate 77 Penny Red, worth a whopping £550,000

2. 1904 Edward VII 6d pale dull purple, sold for over £400,000

3. 1978 Roses error stamp, worth £130,000

4. 1840 Penny Black, can fetch £46,000

5. 1884 Brown-Lilac, an impressive £20,000

Your stamps don't need to be super rare to be worth money, though. Here are a few stamps that anyone could have at home without even knowing it:

> 1840 Penny Blacks are more common than you think and whilst those in mint condition will bring the eye-watering figure above, some of the damaged ones are still highly sought and can bring several hundred pounds, rising to several thousand.

> 1840 Two Penny Blue stamps are quite common and can net you anything from £15 to £50, dependant

on quality. Any rare additions could be worth several hundred pounds.

> Queen Elizabeth II error stamps. Throughout her reign, various printing errors occurred which has resulted in high values. Depending on the mistakes, these can be worth anything from £50 to several thousand.

As we have discussed, it can be difficult to get a valuation, so here are my top tricks and tips to best understand the value of your stamp collection.

> Visit the UK's largest national stamp show, Stampex, and get some sound expert advice on how much your stamps could be worth. This event usually takes place annually in September.

> Contact the Philatelic Traders' Society to find out information on your local dealers. Contact a couple to obtain prices. You will be under no obligation to sell and can use this as a base to set a price if you do.

> eBay is the jack of all trades auction site and it has loads of listings of stamps, so trawl through them to get a sense of value based on current listings and recently sold prices.

> Many auction houses have a past results section on their website and may have held specific stamp auctions in the past, so take a look at the previous results to find out how much your stamp could go for.

Coins

There are some fantastic and wildly exaggerated myths surrounding coins and their value. I've seen some coins put up for sale on various online sites for tens of thousands of pounds more than they are worth.

The truth is that most coins are only worth the value that they represent. Many of us collect coins; in fact, according to the Royal Mint, they are the second most collected item in the UK. Coins are accessible, we all handle them day in day out and we could have some in our pockets and purses right now that could be worth big money to a collector. We don't have to have a collection to make money from coins, especially the most collectible of them all, the 50p piece.

Like stamps, the value of your coins will depend on their age, rarity, material used to manufacture, mistakes and condition. Just for fun let's take a look at some of the world's most expensive coins before we move on to the coins that you could have lying around.

> The 1794 Flowing Hair silver dollar sold for $10 million

> The 1787 Brasher Doubloon sold for $7.4 million

> The 723 Umayyad gold dinar sold for £3.7 million

> The 1343 Edward III florin sold for £480,000

For the purpose of looking into coins that you may have on you right now, that could yield a decent profit, I am going to concentrate on 50p coins as they are the UK's most collected coin.

The fascination with this coin has always bubbled away in the background but it captured most of our imaginations and hearts with the limited edition 2012 Olympic coins that were released. The larger size and the shape of this coin mean that detailed images for limited edition coins can be showcased.

As a little word to the wise, this list is not extensive or exclusive; there are lots more coins worth decent money and I will give you tips later on how to find out if yours are amongst them.

> Kew Gardens 50p piece. This is the holy grail of 50p pieces. Used ones can go for around £140 but some of the uncirculated ones can reach in excess of £900. With 210,000 produced you could be in with a chance of finding one.

> There were 1,225,212 Triathlon 50p coins made so likelihood is that you have already used one without even knowing. These sell for £35.

> There were 1,115,500 of the offside rule 50p coins produced. One could net you £75.

> The wrestling coin from the 2012 Olympics is worth around £20 and there were 1,225,212 made.

> The Judo coin from the same Olympics is worth around £30, holding a slightly higher value due to only 1,151,500 having been produced.

> The 2009 Blue Peter 50p can demand anything from £50 to £350, depending on condition.

There are other denominations of coins that might be

worth big money, including some limited edition 10p, £1 and £2 coins. Remember, if you do have any coins with mistakes on them then this could raise their values into the hundreds and sometimes thousands.

There are a couple of easy ways to check the value of your coins:

> eBay – You will see varied prices ranging from pennies to thousands for coins like yours so it can be confusing as to what yours is worth. However if you look at the 'sold' section on the website then you can see exactly what they sold for.

> Change Checker – This is a great resource to help you to identify whether you have any valuable coins lying around in your piggy bank.

> Coin Hunter – This site will help you to understand what coins like yours are selling for.

Toys

This is an extremely large and varied category which would take me years to fully dissect, but it is worth looking at the most popular toys you might have that could be worth the greatest value to a collector:

> Star Wars

> Disney collections

> Barbie dolls

> Hot Wheels

> Action Men

> Furbies

> Beanie Babies

> Lego

These are the toys most likely to make you some money but with the global toy industry valued at over £100 billion, you may well have something that's of value to a collector out there. Particularly when you consider that a recent study found that almost half of adults still have toys from their childhood. So, it's worth investing the time to check what you have and see whether it could be a collection for cash.

There are many adult collectors of toys and they are fascinating and passionate people. I once presented a TV item where we met some adult collectors of Barbie, Sindy and Action Man. All of them were collectors as children but stopped when they became teenagers. They then rekindled their love for toys and collections in adulthood, some stating that escapism or nostalgia reignited their passion. All of which aligns with my theory that collectors often do so in order to evoke a feeling of happiness and familiarity.

Some of the most valuable toys you could have in your collection are:

> A pristine condition original Barbie could be worth £25,000.

> A faulty Gobbles the Beanie Baby sold for £17,500.

> Some Pokémon cards from the 1990s sell for £1,000 upwards.

The toy collecting community is vast and a wonderfully

inclusive space which welcomes new people with open arms, so obtaining prices can be pretty easy. I find joining as many toy collecting communities that are relevant to the toys you want to sell is the easiest way to value what you have. They are full of experts within their own field who will have a clear knowledge of what price tag you can add to your old toys. Not only this, but quite often it means a direct link to buyers, so you could potentially value and sell your old toys in one.

You can also try visiting a local auction house. They will offer free valuations on all your toys and you are under no obligation to sell with them. They do charge a fee to put your item into auction so always find out what this is. However, if you'd rather do the leg work yourself, you can look to sell via other methods I will come onto shortly.

Other collectibles

Some other collections you could have at home that could bring in the cash:

> Art and paintings

> Antique furniture

> Ornaments

> Tea sets

> Dinner sets

> Wine and whisky

> Vinyl

> Movie memorabilia

> Sports memorabilia

> Royal memorabilia

Although I haven't been able to list every single type of collection and every single item with a market amongst collectors, I hope you are starting to realise that collections and collectibles can bring you some big money. Remember, you can sell a full collection as a job lot but you can make anywhere from 10–40 per cent more if you have the time and energy to sell your collectibles individually.

With regards to selling your items and how. you have plenty of options at your disposal:

Selling via forums and groups

If you are joining groups and forums to value your items, why not use these platforms and contacts to help sell your items? You can advertise what you have to sell and interested collectors can make bids. I find that this is a way to obtain a fair price as you will most probably have more than one or two bidders, and with an open forum of likeminded collectors, this can be conducted in the most transparent way.

As with all online sales, caution is advised and please check and adhere to all rules, regulations and guidelines that the admin for the groups will have in place.

eBay

I say it a lot, but there's a reason that it's the second most visited online marketplace in the world, operating in more than 190 markets globally. Therefore, eBay is a fantastic way to reach a vast number of collectors, but make sure you do a lot of research prior to putting your item up for sale and ensure that you take clear pictures with good descriptions in order to stand out from the crowd. Remember that fees apply.

Etsy

This is a site that attracts enthusiasts and you will find that anyone wishing to buy all or part of your collection will have a good knowledge of the item you are trying to sell, so be prepared for some technical and advanced questions. Fees vary on this site depending on the sale item but collectibles and collections sell very well here.

Auctions

I would generally suggest auctions for the higher end collections you may have. Two of my favourites are Tennants in the north or Sotheby's down south. Fees at auctions can be quite substantial, around 15 per cent of the hammer price plus 20 per cent VAT and an additional 1.5 per cent for insurance. You may also have to pay for catalogue pictures. What you lose in percentages you often gain in your items being exposed to an international client base. These auction houses often have categorised sales so that your items can be placed into a specialist auction targeting the specific demographic of buyers looking for what you want to sell.

If you have items that you know have sold in auctions previously but are not the high value pieces I am talking about above, then I would look to more community-based auction houses local to your area.

A little-known secret is that you can sometimes negotiate the fees that auction houses charge. If you have a high value item, it's always worth putting your bartering skills into action to see if an auction house can improve their terms for you. But I wouldn't be cheeky enough to try this if you only have a couple of items or if you know your collection isn't worth a lot.

Contact reputable dealers

There are hundreds if not thousands of potential dealers you can contact to sell your collectibles. Ask the online groups you've joined for recommendations for reputable ones or contact the relevant trade bodies specifically associated with your item(s). You'll likely have to take a hit on your price but once a dealer has taken your collection, the money is yours and the responsibility is all on them to try and flog it.

Fairs and exhibitions

Attending these will allow you to network and find enthusiasts who will be interested in your collection. You also have the added buzz of the event that will get people excited and more likely to pay a premium. Some events allow you to set up a stall and sell but if not you can set up some deals on the sidelines with like-minded people.

As a history enthusiast and collector myself, I absolutely love the art of collecting, the world and the people who inhabit it. I sincerely hope you find out why I am so passionate about this money-making activity and, I assure you, you'll have loads of fun when you embrace it.

BARGAIN FINDS FOR BIG BUCKS

Once when I was promoting my TV show *Million Pound Pawn*, I explained to a journalist that my true passion was to help others achieve their money-making potential. I explained that I had the money-making tips and tricks to help anyone make money from their 'bubble'. The journalist didn't seem convinced so I told her, 'If you give me £10, I can turn that into hundreds of pounds,' and that all I would need was access to some charity shops. Consumer journalism is huge, so Susan, the journalist who was speaking to me from the *Sun* newspaper, couldn't resist the opportunity to see if I could meet this challenge.

We met up one morning and over the space of a couple of hours, I set about the charity shops choosing one bargain after another, selling them to clients along the way until I had flipped deals starting from £10, turning that tenner into nearly £1,200.

How did I achieve this, I can hear you ask. Well, I picked an affluent area (Chiswick, West London) because the likelihood is that the items within a charity shop here will be worth more money, and then I went about my hunt.

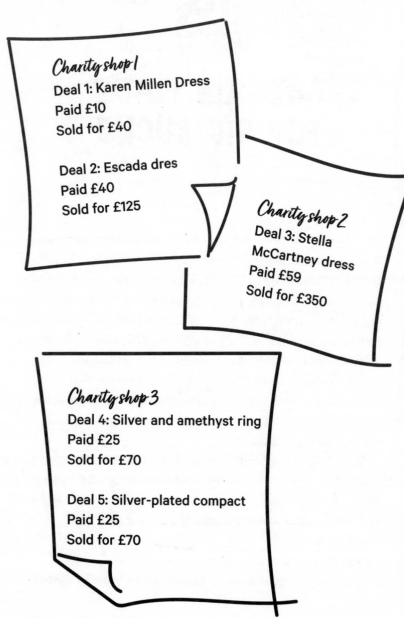

Charity shop 1
Deal 1: Karen Millen Dress
Paid £10
Sold for £40

Deal 2: Escada dres
Paid £40
Sold for £125

Charity shop 2
Deal 3: Stella McCartney dress
Paid £59
Sold for £350

Charity shop 3
Deal 4: Silver and amethyst ring
Paid £25
Sold for £70

Deal 5: Silver-plated compact
Paid £25
Sold for £70

Charity shop 4
Deal 6: Eley Kishimoto
sunglasses
Paid £32
Sold for £90

Charity shop 5
Deal 7: Hermes scarf
Paid £125
Sold for £250

Charity shop 6
Deal 8: Silver cheese knive
Paid £20
Sold for £120

Deal 9: Gold antique broac
Paid £140
Sold for £250

Deal 10: Make leather
jacket
Bought £40
Paid £350

My total profit worked out at **£1,199.**

Now, I'm not suggesting for one minute that I can help everyone achieve such a profitable transformation in a couple of hours. It has taken me over 20 years to know what items can sell for a profit, what brands to look out for and to build up a network of keen buyers who are often happy to do deals with me so immediately. But it does prove to you that there is money to be found within bargains and that if I share all my knowhow with you, soon enough you can be visiting charity shops and second-hand emporiums to bag yourself a bargain that you can transform into big bucks.

To evaluate whether there is money to be made from your bargain finds, you will need to follow my four simple steps:

Step 1 – Is there a demand?

A simple question. You may find similar items listed for sale but do they sell and how often? A bargain is only a bargain in this case if it can be flogged quickly. We don't want your money tied up in loads of items; we want to spin our cash, make it work for us to make more money. Look at past sales results on various platforms to see if there is demand: eBay is particularly useful for this level of research.

Step 2 – Does the price reflect the condition and edition?

Almost everything will sell but how much it will sell for often depends on the quality of the product. Is it scratched? Does it need some repair work? Also, is this a limited edition product that could be sold for more or is it mass produced and easily acquired? Understanding these factors and how they affect what price you can charge will inform you of the amount you should pay to acquire it.

Step 3 – Factor in costs

Selling and buying is great business, but you have to cost up the entire process to ensure you aren't eating into your profit margins. These are the areas to consider the costs associated with selling:

> The cost of delivery or for you to pick up the item.

> The percentage or fee that you may have to pay to sell the item on a specific platform.

> Adverting and marketing costs.

> Costs to bring the item to market, such as any repairs, refurbishment or cleaning fees.

> Any additional costs to store the item or insure it whilst it's in your possession.

> Any taxes or duty that need to be paid on the item (especially look out for this when buying or selling internationally).

> Accountancy and account filing costs. Although hard to attribute the specific cost per item, you should consider these costs when undertaking resell activities if they apply to you.

Adding up all these costs will help you to determine if you can make a profit.

Step 4 – Is it worth it?

After we take all of the above into account, we are better informed as to what an item might sell for, but don't forget to value your time. It is going to take you hours of labour to get your bargains to market, so consider the time you will have to spend to:

> Take pictures to advertise the goods.

> Write descriptions and upload listings onto various platforms.

> Answer questions from potential buyers.

> Package up the items and post them.

With an overview of all these elements you can decide – it is worth it?

Dan's Top Tip

Your time should always be worth the current minimum hourly wage. Anything more is a bonus but if you can't earn that you should find another money-making activity.

If after following my four simple steps, you conclude that there are big bucks to be found within bargains, we can begin. But a word of warning: this process is about investment and reward. We're not utilising the stuff we have lying around your home or using your hobbies to turn a profit; the art of spotting a bargain to resell requires some of your hard-earned cash in the first place.

The good news is that you don't need a massive bank

account balance to bank roll this money-making activity. Like I did in the charity shops, you can start with as little as £10 and still start flipping into profit before you know it.

It is so easy to get carried away and spend loads of your own money to buy items from various outlets, believing that you are going to make a fortune overnight. Often, you will see bargains that are attractive to your personal taste and think because you like them, loads of people will. But this is a dangerous path to walk. Your personal taste could blind you from seeing what the true value of an item is, so remember to leave your emotions at the door and think like a bubble entrepreneur who is ready to make some money.

Start your reselling career small and narrow. By that, I mean have a strategy of what you want to resell and pick a category to start off with. Buy one or a couple of items first to gently test the water and get a better understanding of whether your strategy is going to be profitable. This will also build up your knowledge and confidence quickly, limiting any potential loss of money.

My best way to help you decide this is to imagine you were going on *Mastermind*, the TV show. Each contestant picks a very specific category which is extremely precise, like 'Henry VIII gout attacks' – well, that would be my specialist subject anyway. If you are interested in and knowledgeable about jewellery, maybe start with silver rings and chains. This will help to focus your thinking so that you can research this one area to understand the market, what is and isn't on trend, and cross-reference loads of ecommerce sites to get a picture of sales histories of similar items.

Charity shops

Once you have picked your category, is it time to go bargain hunting. Charity shops are steeped in the history of the British high street, but the perception of them has changed drastically over the last two decades. When I was growing up, it was deemed pretty cheap to be seen in a charity shop. That somehow these places were only for those at the lowest socio-economic level of society. It was ridiculous how anyone could have such a negative image of a place where you could find brilliant bargains which in turn made your money stretch further. But I was a child of the 1980s, a time when consumerism increased and conspicuous consumption (buying expensive stuff to show other people how well you are doing) was raging.

Nowadays, being thrifty, attempting to find bargains, and making money from things others throw away are all celebrated; we marvel at hearing people turn pennies into pounds, and let's not forget how this practice helps sustainability and drives down the need to manufacture more. We are living in an era that has undergone what many call the 'Aldification' effect – whereas once, a large proportion of people wouldn't want to be seen in stores selling cheaper items like Aldi, now, if you aren't going to these places then many people will mock you for spending over the odds for no real reason. It's a full circle moment which is better for us all and our pockets.

Ultimately, charity shops are wonderful places not only to support particular good causes but also to find bargains which you can turn into profit. With over 11,000 charity shops across the country, there are rich pickings to be had.

The location of a charity shop and other second-hand stories is vital. Where they are located determines what type of items will have been donated or sold to the store. I look at leafier suburbs for my charity shop finds. An area with a concentrated high-earning demographic will always have the potential for some wonderful goods. I often find that the stores in the wealthier postcodes will carry designer goods, jewellery and other treasures. Whatever the reason, wealthier areas and those with an older demographic generally donate a lot of their unwanted goods to charity shops, which means you are more likely to find a bargain.

I suggest finding the more boutique charity shops on the outskirts of big cities or in some of the beautiful towns we have across our nation.

My top five areas for charity shops are:

1. **Chiswick in west London**

   A leafy and wealthy suburb. You will find a selection of wonderful shops on the high street. Turn down Turnham Green Terrace and you will find more charity shops filled to the brim with designer goodies at a fraction of the cost.

2. **Nottingham**

   With around 100 charity shops within 5 miles of the city centre, this is known as the charity shop capital of the UK.

3. **Bournemouth**

   Consistently in the top three when it comes to the number of charity shops per capita. Try Winton high street for some great bargains.

4. **Edinburgh**

   Lots of high-end items can be found in Scotland's capital. Head over to the Newington area for some serious finds.

5. Harrogate

A favourite destination for me when it comes to sourcing some bargains. This is a stunning spa town with plenty of wealth, which is reflected in the type of items that you can find here. I have heard from various bargain seekers that jewellery can often be found worth many times more than the amount asked.

As you can see from my top areas, you are going to have to be prepared to travel to find the best bargains. Though smaller towns may also have a charity shops containing a load of items that can be turned in to profit. I regularly visit quaint, sleepy towns in middle-class areas and find fantastic designer goods to flip.

I often hear people say 'I never find a bargain in a charity shop' or something to that effect and it's usually because they are not a frequent visitor. The wonderful thing about a charity shop is that stock comes and goes constantly; donations are continuous and so an item that wasn't there when you first visited could be sitting pride of place when you go again. So, the key to buying items to sell on for profit from charity shops is frequency. You have to visit several times a week. With these shops, very often the saying 'the early bird catches the worm' is true. Staff will often restocked items in the morning, so try to get there early to find your treasured bargains.

But is searching charity shops to turn a profit ethical? This is a question I hear often. It's one I have asked myself and I have put to many volunteers at charity shops, and I am yet to have anyone tell me they think it is a bad thing. Ultimately, they are more than happy to see people coming into their stores to purchase things and sell them on. After all, charity shops exist to fund charities, so the more they make, the more the charity will make.

One lovely assistant in a store in Chiswick pulled out a jacket from the back to tell me that I could make a few hundred pounds if I resold the item. I once wrote on my social media about making profit from charity shop finds to a response of, 'This is music to my charity shop manager ears.' I've been told that the main objective for the charity shop is turnover; many want to keep moving stock and the stark reality is that customers are only willing to pay a certain amount for items from a charity shop. This may have to do with the preconceptions we've had about these stores over the decades, I am not entirely sure, but the reality is that we expect bargains in charity shops.

Most charity shop managers are highly experienced and know the value of the items in front of them, but they also understand the limits of what people are willing to pay – remember, this was donated to them, so any profit is a positive. Many stores have someone who can identify the sought-after or higher value items, but to sell them on the sites we have discussed, where they could potentially make more money, would require more time and manpower.

Unsatisfied, though, that I would have any right to tell people if they were OK to find bargains in charity shops to resell, I contacted the Charity Retail Association for comment and Robin Osterley, Chief Executive, responded: 'Whilst it's not something we would actively encourage or promote, we do recognise that reselling happens and of course it does generate sales for our members – it's all part of the rich tapestry of charity shops. We are here to promote charity retailers and encourage best practice when it comes to pricing items, so that they can maximise the returns for their parent charities. At the moment reselling appears not to be adversely affecting charity shop sales, but we would encourage resellers to think carefully about any impact it might have in the future, particularly where items are resold at a very considerable profit.'

If I have secured an absolute bargain from a charity shop, I will often donate some of my profit to the charity associated with the shop I got it from.

Charity shops can be wonderful places to pick items up for resale but there are other places you can find a bargain to turn it into big bucks.

Car boot sales

I'm sure by now you know how much I love a car boot. But these places aren't just great for selling your items, they are also amazing for sourcing items. The difference here is that a car boot can often feel very busy and pressurised. Everybody is looking for a bargain and it can feel overwhelming. It is vital that you have some sort of structure or plan in place prior to visiting a car boot. Remember: buy in haste and you'll repent in leisure when you can't flog the item on for a profit.

My top tips for sourcing bargains at a car boot:

Only buy a few items to begin with
Remember one of my four simple steps: have a category when first starting out. If your aim, for example, is to buy kids items then be focused on toys and clothing. Prior to visiting the car boot, research what is selling well in this area, write down all the brands to look out for, go on forums

on Facebook and other platforms and look at what items within this category people are searching for.

The more experienced you get, the more categories you might be comfortable with, but whilst you're a newbie, I don't want you to feel overwhelmed or delve into areas you don't necessarily have a breadth of knowledge in.

Look at weather reports

We live in the UK and the weather is unpredictable, so check the reports the day before. Also look at any groups or forums that may be following or reporting on the car boot that you plan to attend. The last thing that you want to do is to travel somewhere only to be told that it's not happening. That will cost you money and time, two things we could always do with more of, so don't waste them by not being vigilant.

Bring lots of change and money

Most traders will not have the facility to take card payments. Having a load of change in your pocket can also work as an excellent bartering tool. Say something is £8 but you have exactly £6.50 in your pocket and you show the cash in your palm, it's much more likely that you will have your cheeky offer accepted. When someone physically sees the money and knows that they won't have to use their float to give you change, it's a much more powerful bargaining tip than many people realise. Also, take your own carrier bags. Pulling one out whilst trying to barter for an item and saying something like 'you don't even need to give me a bag I've brought my own' seems like it would be a throwaway comment, but it gives you a slight edge and breaks down barriers of formality.

Don't just browse, dig deep

I often see people at car boots just surface gaze – by which I mean they don't look in boxes and bargain bins; instead, they just browse. You won't have exposure to all of the amazing treasures that could be lurking around if you don't get stuck in and dig deep.

Examine items carefully

If you think you've found something that will sell well and make a decent profit, it is really important to inspect the item thoroughly. If it's electrical proceed with caution; ask if the stall owner has a power supply to test the item. Remember once the deal is done and the day is over the likelihood of you getting your money back is slim to none. The items at a car boot are bought as seen.

Seasonality

When it comes to seasons, the opposite method should be applied when buying a bargain. You'll remember that I always advocate to sell for the season you are in – but flip this on its head when buying. You'll get some lucrative deals if you can buy out of season at the car boot. This is because most people there are buying for need, but you're buying to flip. So in the heat of summer, a seller isn't going to get rid of that winter coat to most buyers. Therefore, offer low and you'll likely bag a massive bargain.

Then, all you need to do is store it for a couple of months and be prepared to reap the rewards of the demand by supplying the goods at the right month.

Facebook Marketplace

This is a great and broad place to buy bargains. There can be quite a lot of items that would be hard to sell on for a profit due to their condition or the price that the sellers want; however, there is treasure within. The key to any marketplace is bartering and you can really give it a good go on these sites, trying to get the sellers as low as possible. The great thing is that if you're not quite ready to barter on price face to face, this is another opportunity to perfect your 'art of the barter' as it is all done online via Messenger, but my guidelines on how to conduct yourself still apply, just because you are behind a computer screen does not give you a right to be rude or inappropriate.

Some other places you can try to secure a bargain:

> Gumtree

> Depop

> Auctions (but remember there is a buyer's fee added on top of the hammer price, so work the total cost out before agreeing to a sale.)

It is near impossible to give you a definitive list of what to invest in for your resale journey, but I'd say it is worth paying particular attention to items that are often overlooked. Once you've completed your evaluation of demand for items, this will help guide you. Items I have seen undervalued within charity chops and other second-hand sales outlets include:

> Books, especially limited and first editions

> Clothing, especially clothes from the 1990s and 2000s (I see these reselling on Vinted for serious cash)

> Children's toys. Most sell well but older classics can attract a really good price. This includes:

  • Barbie, Sindy and Action Man

  • Beanie Babies

  • Polly Pockets

  • Furbies

  • Computer consoles and games

  • Board games (when complete with all components)

  • Lego

> Baby items such as cots and prams

> Retro and vintage furniture.

Now that you know where to source your items, we need to look at how and where best to sell them.

This chapter is different to most within *Money Maker* because you have had to invest an initial outlay to try and secure a profit through re-sales. Due to this, I want us to focus our sales strategy on free platforms where you won't have to pay any commission.

Facebook fan groups

These can be a great place to re-sell your bargain finds. If your item is collectable, valuable or attractive to enthusiasts, then online forums dedicated to the type of item you have to sell can be a great place to start. If, for instance, you have a couple of Barbies you want to sell, we know that this is an iconic brand and so there will be thousands of fantastic online groups and forums dedicated to her.

As discussed in the previous chapter, connecting with enthusiasts is beneficial on so many levels: not only are you directly accessing potential buyers, you are also meeting people who have specialist knowledge and understanding of the item you want to sell. You will not be able to pull the wool over their eyes, so when dealing with fans and enthusiasts, be respectful as they will likely have a better understanding of the item's worth than you do. Embrace this, allow the discussions to help you get a better understanding of your item and what you can sell it for – but always get a second opinion.

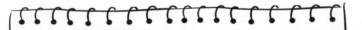

Dan's Top Tip

Be extra vigilant when selling on forums and fan groups as often these sites are run by volunteers, so you have little protection when parting with your item. Ensure a safe and secure way to exchange the payment for the product.

Remember, this community most probably wants your item, so don't be fooled by their knowledge and blindsided into a cheap sale.

You can still sell via Facebook groups if your item isn't a collectable. There will be groups and forums, based around a geographical location too, like 'Sheffield buy and sell'. These groups are great place to sell generic, everyday items like tools, furniture, electronics and other household items.

Follow my six-step guide to successful selling to Facebook groups:

> Find the group you want to join, read the description of the group and their terms and conditions, and, if you agree with it all, join or ask to join.

> Join as many groups as possible. If your item is a collectible or somethings that enthusiasts will be keen to snap up, the likelihood is that there will be multiple groups, so spread your bets and engage with as many as possible to prompt a quicker sale and possibly even a bidding war.

> Immerse yourself in the conversation and ask questions. Engaging with these groups not only drums up interest in what you have to sell but can give you answers to questions you may have to help you determine the price of your item. I can pretty much tell you the price of a piece of gold from touch but Hot Wheels toy cars I would have to research. So enjoy the process of finding out from the people who adore these various items but always get multiple guides on price to ensure a solid sale.

> Post the sale item on all the relevant groups you

have joined. Upload lots of clear pictures which best showcase your item, write a thorough and detailed description and be transparent about any flaws, defects or issues. The more information you give, the less likely you'll have to spend lots of time answering questions from buyers.

> Treat everyone with respect, be polite and courteous. You only sell as well as your brand and if you're known to be difficult or rude, word will spread and your retail dreams of turning bargains into big bucks will be scuppered.

> Bring out your bartering skills to turn a profit. People on online forums and groups looking to buy will be experienced and want to get a bargain. So have your negotiating prowess turned up a notch and be prepared to haggle and stay strong on the price you want to achieve.

Facebook Marketplace

In addition to Facebook groups and forums, there is Facebook Marketplace which is vast in size and reach making, it a top-choice platform for buying and selling second-hand goods. We've discussed how to buy on here, so similar guidelines apply if you want to use this platform to sell.

Personally, I find that selling on Facebook Marketplace works best if you live in a city or large town, as you will have a broader customer base and you can also advertise that your item is for collection only and therefore save on P&P. If you exchange locally and don't use the payment processing built within marketplace, you also save on any system fees.

If you are security conscious or simply don't want people to know your home address, then agree to meet a buyer in a public place which is well populated. Take a friend with you for extra security and if payment hasn't been transferred securely already, obtain the cash before you part with the goods. This platform is designed to facilitate local transactions and direct purchases within your own community.

We discussed how you can optimise your sales of collectibles by using Facebook groups and forums, but outside of this I wouldn't suggest Facebook Marketplace for high-value items. It is a brilliant community-based resource that helps people to make money for their unwanted items, which means more unused items can be reused and repurposed, which I love. But if you snagged a high-value item when bargain hunting, you should consider the best place to sell it. This might lead you to a specialist sales site, which will want to take a commission, which we may often prefer to avoid so as not to dent our profits, but, for assurance that you are protected from any scams and are securing a legitimate sale, it may be worthwhile. Explore a couple of options and ask for the best deals on commission – don't be afraid to use sites against each other. If your item is of high value, the likelihood is that they'll lower their rates if you tell them their opposition has offered you better terms.

Now, let's get back to the best way to sell your bargain finds on Facebook Marketplace.

> First things first, log in to your Facebook account (or create one if you don't already have one) and click on the marketplace icon, followed by the selling icon and finally choose 'create new listing'. Then you will need to choose the listing type, which is currently

separated into three categories: items, vehicle and property (for sale or rent).

> Once you've clicked on the type of item for sale (I doubt any of you found a vehicle or property in the charity shop, but if you did, tell me your secret), you need to create your listing. Upload as many clear pictures from various angles as possible. You can even upload a video to showcase the great quality and look of what you are selling. Write a title that's as descriptive as possible, input the price making sure you have done your research to price yourself in the most attractive way, select the category of your item from the dropdown menu and then highlight the condition from the dropdown menu. There are just three options here, so if your item has seen better days, be honest in the 'more details' section, where you can supply further information.

> Choose your location, though don't give you exact address. If you're in a large city perhaps include your borough or general neighbourhood so that people can decide if you are too far away.

> You will then have the option to post your listing to any groups that you are a member of. Only choose the groups that are relevant to this particular item. If you have separately advertised to a group before creating a listing, do not share it to this group again as members don't like it.

> Hit the publish button to start selling.

Once the listing is active you can monitor how it is doing by clicking the 'your items' tab to see any activity around the item. Any direct messages about the listing will come through to your Messenger, so don't forget to keep an eye on this.

I have said this before and I will say it again but please put your safety first. This is paramount and there is no amount of money in the world worth jeopardising your safety. Here are some tips:

> Scammers exist, so proceed with caution. I have seen lots of scams where fake emails or images are used to try to convince the seller that payment has been approved. Use trusted and secure online payment systems or, better still, deal in cash.

> Research your buyer. Look at their profile to see what they post and who they interact with to better understand who you are dealing with. I have on many occasions asked for proof of ID from a person before agreeing to meet with them. If their driving licence or passport doesn't match their profile, find out why. This isn't full proof but asking for this can often scare off scammers.

> Be confident to walk away. If you get a bad feeling about anyone or start to feel uneasy or pressured, just walk away. Tell the interested party that the item has sold and is no longer available.

> Set a time limit. I've seen listings drag on for ages and have also encountered fake buyers who assure you they want an item only to ghost you. Once you've agreed a sale with someone, set a 48-hour

time limit for them to purchase and collect the item. If they don't come through, you can move on to the next potential buyer.

> Meet in safety. Only meet in places you know, that are well populated and safe. Take a friend or family member with you as an extra precaution. Don't ever hand over any goods without having secured payment. People may ask to do a final check of the item which could be a scam to run away with it.

Other online marketplaces

Some other sites where it is free to sell your bargain finds include:

Gumtree
This was the first online classifieds platform in the UK. You don't get charged a fee for selling on this platform. Designed to connect people within communities who can help each other with specific needs, in recent years, they have made an active effort to restore the community ethos and environment which was fundamental from the site's inception.

Shpock
This platform is easy to use and fast becoming a very popular place to sell second-hand items. Like many online marketplaces, they support local trading, building a community for buyers and sellers to connect. There are no selling fees (except for cars) and with over 12 million monthly users, you are likely to find buyers quickly.

Whilst there are places where you can sell your bargain finds without paying commission, there are also ways to secure items for free that you can turn into a profit. Facebook Marketplace, Gumtree and plenty of others list items that people just want to get rid of. On top of this, I've known many a person dumpster dive for hidden treasure they can turn into big bucks.

Now, I am not advising any of you to go out and jump into skips, but legally, as long as a bin or skip is on public land and not locked, then it is generally OK to take items from it which you could upcycle or sell on. Hopefully, it goes without saying but please be safe if you ever decide to do this.

MOONLIGHT
FOR MONEY

Life is expensive and gone are the days where we could all rely on our job to cover the entire cost of living. Sorry to sound bleak, but I believe in facing the facts head-on if we are going to make positive changes to our own lives.

I'm seeing a big change in the relationship between our earning ability and the everyday cost of living. It's costing more to produce and taxes are rising; therefore, our ability to buy the things we want is inhibited. For many of us, the simple truth is we can't afford to buy as much and the luxury treats in life like a meal at a restaurant are less frequent as a result.

All of this feeds into exactly why I wanted to write this book, why I want to show you how to release your money-making potential and get back the things, however big or small, you deserve. Some people might think a solution to higher prices is to stop doing the things you once loved, to cut back or lower your standard of living – but this goes against the very fibre of my being. I want you to have everything you desire and I want to do all that I can to help you achieve that. It's going to take some elbow grease but with a little extra work, you can soon be achieving the lifestyle you deserve.

We've discussed renting and selling your belongings to plug the financial gap, but these aren't the only solutions. I want to introduce you to the wonderful world of side hustles, a concept now so popular within society that, according to finder.com, 44 per cent of Brits are doing it.[11] A staggering 76 per cent of this figure is made up of under-25s, all of them hustling their way to financial freedom.[12] Gen Z is embracing and adapting this approach, finding ways to get the life they want, setting trends and showing us the importance of the side hustle.

It is thought that almost 50 per cent of the population will be undertaking a side hustle by 2025, which is a 40 per cent increase from 2017, and that, Brits could earn up to a whopping £10,000 a year in additional income from side hustles.[13] If that figure is true, that means we could all be earning £192 extra a week. I don't know about you, but that sounds very good to me.

So, let's first understand what a side hustle is. Quite simply, it's a secondary revenue stream that people look at to top up their earnings alongside their primary way of making money – although you could undertake multiple side hustles to form your entire earning potential, instead of one job. There are many side hustles that you can find and develop, and we will discuss a lot of them later. Let's begin by taking a look at some of the top-earning side hustles according to Materials Market:

> Dropshipping is like a digital shop front window but you don't have the items in stock (on your person). Instead, you order them direct from the supplier once you have received a customer order. Can make you £1,300 per calendar month (pcm).

> Baking is a very profitable side hustle which could earn you £1,000 pcm.

> Pet sitting is another valuable one that could earn you £430 pcm, but has the potential for you to earn a lot more.

Focus groups and surveys

Side hustles come in all shapes and sizes, with the knowledge or skill level varying dependant on what you want to do. A pretty simple side hustle to get into is being paid for your opinion. Yes, that's right, you can be paid for giving your thoughts on all sorts of things – it might be the taste of a new chocolate bar, the experience of playing a computer game or even sampling and testing new beauty products from the comfort of your own home.

It is believed that internet searches for online focus groups have increased by 184 per cent in the last year, which is unsurprising as you can be paid serious cash for your opinions on companies, products and services. You don't need any experience as you are literally being asked your opinion on something they share with you and you could earn around £25–£50 per hour.

Marketing and targeting the right demographic are so important to companies and their profit margins, which makes surveys an integral way for these businesses to create their future strategy. This is so easy for anyone to do at home and it's a much more relaxed way of giving your opinions compared to focus groups, although you often don't get paid as much for your time. To get started, all you have to do it sign up to a couple of websites that offer to pay you for completing surveys and then you can start earning anything from £5 to £20 for each one you do.

There are also focus groups which you need to attend in person. I think they are a great side hustle if you have the means to travel. It's a varied market so you could be asked your opinion on current affairs, to eat new food samples or even be paid to watch television. The list is pretty endless but do read the small print as I have seen many of these companies pay you in vouchers. The vouchers are accepted in major high street chains around the country, but if you need cold, hard cash from your side hustle, check this is an option first.

Below are six companies that have in-person focus groups (they also offer online) that I think are worth the effort:

1. Saros Research is by far one of the most established in this market. This company works with some of the biggest household brands and could see you tasting and reviewing new drinks, snacks and food. They also work with fashion, furniture and supermarket brands, as well as tech companies, so you can expect a varied way to earn extra money. You can earn £40–£100 for an hour's work on average, so there is a lot of potential to build up a very lucrative side hustle here.

2. Trend Market Research has an impressive track record with lots of interesting past projects and some very

fun-sounding future ones. You can get paid to try out walking boots and even earn by ordering coffee from different cafes. Projects usually range from £50 to £200 for a few hours work. I think the variation of this company and the testing you might participate in feels like you wouldn't see this as work.

3. QMR Recruitment is another with lots of variation that will keep you entertained with focus groups, creative workshops, product testing and online panels. They aren't as lucrative as some of the others I've seen as you earn roughly £45-plus for a focus group lasting approximately two hours.

4. Research Opinions have some pretty tasty offers when it comes to focus groups, which can earn you £50–£200 per project.

5. Angelfish Opinions is particularly popular with parents of young children. They do various focus groups, from a 45-minute discussion on toys for £65 or fizzy drinks, and research on children's video content.

6. Theviewers.co.uk really does pay you to watch TV programmes. They put together research panels for broadcasters where you get paid for giving your opinion on a TV show before it has been transmitted to anyone else. I think that this sounds like absolute bliss. There are other companies who also provide this service for your time and you can generally earn about £40 a session.

If this has grabbed you attention, here are a few more research sites you could look into signing up with too:

> Branded Surveys

> Swagbucks

> YouGov

> Market Research 4 U

> Focus Force

These focus groups and survey side hustles are really good fun and simple to participate in. My top tips to make it a money-making success for you are:

> Read the small print and work out exactly what you will earn and if you'll be paid in cash or vouchers. Make sure you understand the time commitment and the activity you will be required to participate in.

> Shop around. There are plenty of companies offering these side hustles, so choose ones that ask you to participate in things that you are interested in.

> Have a dedicated email address just for this side hustle. You will most likely sign up to lots of companies and will receive loads of emails, so keep it separate from the rest of your digital life.

> Don't worry if you don't get picked straight away; you will get your turn.

> Be transparent and honest. The more detailed and useful information you give the more likely you will be used again.

> Don't ever pay a fee to join a research company. None of the reputable ones I have researched require

you to part with your own cash for doing a job for them.

Mystery shopping

Some side hustles sound like utter dreams and mystery shopping has to fall into that category for a lot of us – although for my better half, not so much. There are lots of sites you can register with that require you to shop for various companies and feed back on your experiences. This isn't as straightforward as doing surveys and you'll likely have to do an eligibility test, but if you have a sweet spot for shopping, it's definitely worth a try. The pay isn't the greatest I have seen from side hustles but could earn you a couple of extra thousand a year. On average, you can expect to earn £20 but I have seen some mystery shopping jobs where you can earn £200. These are well suited to people who like an adventure or fun experience where you get some free food and, on occasions, may even get to try a night away at a hotel. But remember:

> Only travel for decent money. Remember you need to be paid minimum wage or over, otherwise it's just not worth it.

> You'll have to write up your experience so only take on these jobs if you are a confident writer.

> You need a smart phone to be able to participate.

> Don't ever pay a signing on fee. Reputable companies won't ask for anything from you because they are making money from the companies that are

paying them to conduct the research.

> This side hustle isn't going to make you rich beyond your wildest dreams, but if you are a keen shopper, it is one of the most fun activities to do for some extra cash.

A couple of companies operating within mystery shopping I can suggest:

IPOS UK

This company advertises some jobs that seem to pay well. My research found that you could earn from £100 to £200 enquiring about services rather than purchasing items.

GBW

The test to become one of their mystery shoppers is quite difficult but worth it as they work with some of the biggest brands in the UK and have loads of jobs up and down the country. The pay works out to be about £20–£40 per job.

There are loads more companies out there that can hire you to do mystery shopping, so if this sounds like a fun side hustle for you, get registered now.

Referrals

Another simple way to earn some extra cash is referrals. In essence, you can get rewarded for introducing someone you know to a company/brand. It's a clever way for companies to attract customers, as research by YouGov into 'global trust in advertising good housekeeping' found that 92 per cent of us trust recommendations from people we know and will spend an average of 200 per cent more than customers that aren't referred. If you do explore this money-making side hustle, please only recommend products, services and goods that you value. There are plenty of companies who offer to reward you for recommendations in various ways (always check each company's specific T&Cs):

> Food delivery companies such as Gousto and Hello Fresh offer various incentives, such as £30 off your next order and big discounts off orders for both you and the person you recommend.

> Financial services and banks offer some really strong incentives for recommendations. For example, at time of writing, The Co-op Bank's refer a friend scheme can earn you £125, although there are stipulations that must be followed. And PayPal has a scheme whereby if you get a friend to sign up and spend £5 you both receive £20. You can refer as many friends as you like.

Other businesses that offer referral schemes that can be worth investigating include:

> Utility companies

> Breakdown services

> TV and mobile providers

I would hazard a guess that most companies will offer some sort of incentive if you refer a friend, so look at all the companies you use and see if you can make some money by referring friends who you know will benefit from joining or using them.

Cashback sites

You can make money simply by sitting on your bum and shopping on the internet. Over the last couple of years, this aspect of making money has exploded and it looks set to continue enjoying a meteoric rise in popularity. It does seem strange, though, doesn't it? To be paid to shop. Even I needed a bit of time to process that and I'm the money-making expert!

What you have to do is buy products or services via a cashback site which will reward you with anything from pennies up to hundreds of pounds, depending on the offer. You'll have to register with these sites but be sure not to sign up with one that asks for an annual subscription. Then you simply search for the company or product you want to purchase from and once the transaction has taken place, the amount of cashback earned will be transferred into your site account. You can then draw that cash out upon completion – but be sure to check the T&Cs carefully. For example, some sites have a threshold you must achieve before you can withdraw.

Sounds like witchcraft but it's pretty straight forward. The sites that you register with get paid to direct customers to certain companies; think of comparison websites or holiday search engines. As the transactions are completed in the digital landscape, companies can track where you were directed from to pay that source. The cashback sites offer you cash rewards to use them in the hope you will become a repeat customer.

I find this a really clever business model which is great for benefiting the consumer, but please make sure that you thoroughly research the deal or product you are looking for and make sure that using a cashback site is the most cost-effective method for you. Don't get swayed by big cashback offers if the outlay of the product you are buying isn't the best value on the market. Shop around to find the cheapest product price with a cashback offer and you'll be onto a winner. As someone who uses these sites regularly, I can assure you that you can earn hundreds a year by simply buying the things you need.

Some of the best cashback offers you can find are:

> Car insurance can earn you around £20.

> Vehicle breakdown cover can reward you with £30 to £140.

> Mobile contracts can earn you between £20 and £100.

> Clothing brands will give you 1 per cent to 10 per cent money back.

> Holiday booking sites offer 1 per cent to 9 per cent cashback.

> Electrical products can make 1 per cent to 15 per cent cashback of the purchase price.

> Home insurance cashback offers can earn you £75.

Capitalise on the fact that there is a lot of competition in this market so companies will be fighting to secure your business. This results in big cashback offers so roll up your sleeves and get surfing to find the top deals that work best for you.

I have researched this area extensively and below are a selection of companies I have used, who offer extremely competitive cashback incentives with a proven track record and a loyal client base.

Top Cashback

This is by far my favourite cashback site, due to the calibre of deals they offer compared to their rivals. I looked at a variety of products and found that four out of five times they achieved the best results. You can withdraw your money or you could opt to increase it by 10 per cent if you choose to take payment as e-vouchers. There is a free membership option or a plus membership at a cost of £5, which offers additional incentives and cash-back offers.

Quidco

Another giant in this sector. I have often seen them with better deals than Top Cashback, making the two companies leading rivals. You can withdraw cash but if you opt to convert it for gift cards they will give you up to 15 per cent more. They also have a free membership option and a premium scheme. The premium membership costs £1 a month and pays up to 10 per cent extra in cashback and 20 per cent in payout bonuses.

With so many companies competing in this marketplace, I strongly suggest that you compare at least four or five and how they might meet your cashback needs. Remember, higher cashback doesn't hold its value if the product or service you are purchasing is the most expensive on the market.

Dan's Top Tip

Only use these sites to purchase things you need and are planning on buying regardless. Spending money on an item you don't need to secure the cashback is counterintuitive and not one of my money-making methods.

Using these sites in conjunction with your normal day-to-day purchases could earn you hundreds of pounds a year. On average, a Quidco user can earn £289 a year whilst a Top Cashback user can achieve up to £345.

Delivery driving

Consumerism is increasing demand for items being delivered directly to your home, so becoming a delivery driver in your spare time is a really interesting side hustle. According to a report from Glassdoor.co.uk, the typical Deliveroo driver gets a salary of £17 per hour and if you did your deliveries on your bike, you'd not only be benefitting your bank balance in your spare time but also your health.

It's simple to become a delivery driver, all you need is:

> A mode of transport

> A smartphone

> › Proof of your right to work in the UK

> › To be 18 years old or above

There are many established companies you could join including, Just Eat, Deliveroo and Uber eats.

Home clearance and decluttering

We discussed how to make money from your home back in Chapter 5, so why not convert this expertise to help others make money from theirs? If, like my husband, you actually enjoy decluttering, you could offer a bespoke service to family, friends and even strangers where you help put their home or just a room/cupboard through a sieve. We know from the stats that every home is sitting on a treasure trove worth thousands, so you could earn a decent side hustle wage from helping others to identify the value within their homes. You could even bundle this service up as a spring clean, where you offer to deep clean, declutter and sell on your customer's unused belongings. I would charge £12–£15 per hour and in addition charge a percentage of the items you identify and sell. The percentage you charge is completely up to you, but if you are identifying the valuables within someone's home and then providing the service to sell them, I wouldn't go below 25 per cent (net profit – so after any fees/commissions you have to pay in order to sell). Plus, at this stage of your money-making journey, you will have already become a trusted seller with strong brand awareness, so this holds a value.

Most people don't have the time or quite simply can't be bothered with this task, so securing 25 per cent of the profit for offering this service, plus the hourly wage, is a really quick money-spinner.

There is also the opportunity to offer this service as a home clearance. The sad reality is that home clearances are a part of life, and you could actually be offering a service that is vital and saves families and friends from the heartache of performing it themselves – but please only do this if you are compassionate with a true desire to help others. It wouldn't surprise me if a decent percentage of the billions of pounds' worth of goods we throw away per year as a nation is due to people not being able to do a thorough house clearance. So not only could you develop this into a good side hustle, you can help families and friends make use of unwanted goods whilst also preventing them from populating waste sites.

Become an extra

A more lighthearted and fun way to earn additional funds is something I did to keep me afloat at uni, which was to become a TV or film extra. I appeared in several TV shows including *Hollyoaks*, *No Angels* and even an advert for the AA. Speaking from experience, it's a really fun way to utilise your spare time – the pay is good, they feed you and, in most situations, cover your travel expenses. There are so many agencies out there and I would suggest joining several to better your chances, but always read the small print to know exactly what you are signing up for and what is expected of you. It can often be long days of hanging around and you aren't necessarily guaranteed your 15 ministers of fame. As with most things, I am not a fan of signing-up fees as, ultimately, whatever you end up doing the company is being paid for providing you, so try to research some prominent extras agencies that don't require a fee. If, however, there is a company you think is a better fit for your needs but they require a sign-up fee, I'd advise never going above £40.

Regardless of which ones you join, your fee is generally the same. From most, you can expect anywhere from £85 upwards.

Pallet flipping

Buying a pallet full of unused or returned goods from a retailer and then selling them on is called pallet flipping and it could make you thousands of pounds.

It can feel a little like a game of roulette because you may not always know exactly what is in the pallet, but you can usually buy the contents for a very small percentage of the retail value. I have to reiterate though – this can be a gamble that doesn't always pay off.

More and more places are offering up pallet sales these days:

> eBay

> Marthill International

> wholesaleclearance.co.uk

> discounthouse.co.uk

The key to being successful with this venture is the same as with all of them: the research. There are a lot of pallets on offer, so I advise that you find ones from retailers that stock things you know about, whether that be tools, technology, child's toys or clothes. If you are familiar with the contents, you will understand the profit margin of what's inside the pallet and the amount you can flip them for.

It sounds simple but you wouldn't believe half the stories I could tell you of some 'Del Boy' wannabes trying to flog items they were clueless about.

Anyway, pallet flipping can be fun and interesting but there is a risk, so just be aware of that.

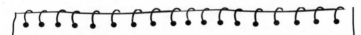

Dan's Top Tip

The key foundation to making money in sales is to know what you are selling and the price it can achieve.

These are just some of the side hustles you can start where you join an organisation, third party or online site to raise extra cash in your spare time. However, some side hustles you could even start from your own skills and hobbies – can you imagine getting paid to do something that brings you joy? Isn't that what we all deserve and aspire to? We often assume that making money can't be fun – it must be hard and tiring. We couldn't possibly enjoy making money, surely? I want you to stop thinking like that! Earning real cash can be incredibly fun, interesting and even easy when you are turning your hobbies into your money-making side hustle.

Let's take a look at some of the most common hobbies and how you can turn them into money-makers for you.

Dog walking and pet sitting

From 2020–22, the UK canine population grew enormously from 9 million to 13 million and roughly 26 per cent of British households have at least one pet cat, which equates to nearly 11 million. Being such a nation of animal lovers means there is demand for people to take care of them. We all have to work and have commitments, but often we don't want that to be to the detriment of our pets, so if you are an animal lover, there are plenty of ways to turn this into a side hustle.

According to Nimblefins, a finance company that conducts research into various topics, the average hourly rate for dog walking is £11.25 per walk (usually 45–60 mins), but location and demand can increase this figure by up to 31 per cent. The basic calculations show that in some circumstances, this could be more than a side hustle and could be a realistic full-time job that might just get you above the national annual salary of £27,756.

Pet sitting is also as lucrative because you can expect to receive between £10 and £15 per visit if you are popping into a client's house to check on a cat or dog. If you are having the cat or dog in your own home, you can charge around £25 to £30 for half a day, £40 for a full day and around £50 for 24 hours.

There are various ways you can get started with a pet walking or sitting side hustle. People are pretty protective of their animals, so trust is key. You could start by offering your services to friends and family, and then slowly broaden this out to the local community. If undertaking this by yourself, rather than working for an established company, you'll need to put some assurances in place and protections for the people leaving their loved ones with you. You can get specific dog walker insurance in the UK for roughly £54 a year or general liability insurance should cover you for pet sitting. Whatever insurance you get, make sure to ask questions and explain fully what you need it for so there are no exclusions that can bite you in the bum later down the line. Also, if you do decide to board dogs at your own home then you will need a licence from your local authority, which will only be granted after thorough checks and site visits to your home; these cost about £250 at present.

Or there are plenty of apps and sites you can join where you will be vetted and can then start your pet-friendly side hustle. You can start your research at:

> care.com

> pawshake.co.uk

> trustedhousesitters.com

> rover.com

Gardening

If you love tinkering around in your garden or allotment, then you could very well have a metaphorical money tree on your hands. Gardening can be the bane of many people's existence so if you have green fingers then this side hustle is for you.

You can start out by just offering to mow lawns. A simple task that many of us dread and lots of us would outsource, providing the price is right. You could also offer to cut hedges, weed and generally tidy up the garden. If you have the skills then offering to plant, prune and take care of flowers could be the next step. Average charges for a gardening service start from £12 per hour and can go up to £59, depending on your location and the service you are providing.

Below is my guide to costing based on an average size garden:

> For weeding a full garden you can charge £40 to £50

> Mowing a lawn can earn you £23 to £35

> Jet washing drive, walls and clearing patio gutters demands about £100 to £130

These are basic services so of course; the more advanced and skill-based gardening service you can offer, the more you can charge. Don't forget to look at other service providers in your area to get a better reflection of fair prices for your geographical location.

A couple more green-fingered side hustles:

> Selling seeds

> Growing and selling plants

> Selling fruit or homemade produce from your garden.

Selling items produced from your garden can be done in a variety of ways, ranging from advertising on social media to gain orders to selling through forums and to family and friends.

House cleaning

I know we touched upon spring cleaning earlier, but that is generally something you don't need regularly, whilst there is a huge demand for weekly house cleaning. You don't need any formal qualification as your ability will be what secures you a regular job and word of mouth recommendations mean others also hire you.

Hourly rates depend on where you are based but £12–£17 is roughly the average and you can easily find out the cost of other cleaners in your area to make sure your pricing is right. Whatever your cleaning ambitions, make sure you have any insurance necessary. It isn't a legal requirement in the UK if you are a sole trader doing it yourself, but if you build a cleaning empire and start to hire others, you will need a form of public liability to begin with. Speak with an insurance specialist for advice if you are going to hire other people to work for you.

Ironing

This could easily be included in house cleaning, but I like ironing whereas I do not like the general house cleaning jobs, so I thought this justified its own section.

You can charge either by the hour, roughly £12–18, or by the weight, £4.50–£5.50 per kilogram, or per item. What you charge exactly depends on what other people are charging for this service in your area – remember, you have to be competitive.

Per item guide rates:

> £4–6 for a double duvet cover

> £2.50–£3.50 for a jumper

> £2–2.50 per shirt

Baking

The baking industry is worth a colossal £7.1 billion, so if you love baking why not have a slice of the pie? You could earn yourself hundreds of pounds a month by indulging in this hobby.

There is no limit to what you could bake to sell – whether you opt to hit the seasonal demands of Christmas, Easter and Halloween, or you might want to capitalise on the birthday cake demand in your area. Maybe there are some baked goods you have perfected over the years or even a few baking recipes you have created yourself. Whatever baking treats you can make, you'll be sure to sell them at a number of local locations such as car boots, school fairs and summer fetes.

In recent years, there has been a sharp rise in local sandwich shops and delis outsourcing the production of baked goods to others. So be sure to check with any local cafes and canteens to find out if they are looking to outsource.

You'll need to be sure of any regulations from your local authority to sell baked goods from your home and also do the research to understand the quantity you can turn over. It's also important to manage your ingredient inventory so that nothing goes to waste or goes out of date (which will cost you money). Price your items at the median level based on the highest and lowest prices in your area.

DIY

According to a survey by Waste Removal Experts, 52 per cent of Brits avoid doing DIY and don't think they have the skill to tackle the simplest of home improvement tasks. The average cost of DIY disasters is £7 billion, according to Aviva, so if you are handy with a hammer and enjoy all the odd jobs around the house, there seem to be plenty of people in need of your skills and they'll pay you a decent wage. Take a look at your local area but an average hourly rate for a handyman is £27, which can obviously increase within the bigger cities.

Photography

If you have a keen eye and are click happy, then taking pictures could make you some easy money. If you currently own a high-quality camera, you can sell various photographs as stock photos.

Alamy is one of the biggest and diverse stock libraries in the world and they pay contributors monthly, with a really clear and straightforward payment structure. If your images are exclusive with Alamy, you earn 50 per cent of sales; non-exclusive makes you 40 per cent of all sales and there is no long-term contract.

Tutoring and eCourses

Online tutoring and creating eCourses is a fantastic way to utilise your qualifications and knowledge whilst making some extra cash. Whether you want to teach something academic, impart your business acumen or teach something creative, tutoring or eCourses are in high demand. I'm a qualified diamond grader and I'm really passionate about teaching people the four c's (carat, colour, clarity and cut) so am currently putting together an eCourse myself. But whatever your passion or knowledge, sharing it with others is a side hustle you may not of thought about.

Depending on the eCourse or tutoring subject, you can expect to earn anything from £20 to £85 per hour. You can register your tutoring availability with sites such as Superprof or First Tutors, or for eCourse creation and support, look at websites like Articulate 360, who help give you the resources to create and manage your courses.

Become a virtual assistant

Demand for flexible virtual assistants (VAs) has soared in recent years because of the many benefits they can provide an individual or company. For some administrative roles, you don't need any experience, but any additional skills you do have could secure you a higher fee per hour. For instance, if I was to hire someone it would be to reply to emails and book in appointments, so all you need are strong organisational skills and a professional disposition. Other clients may require specific technological or software skills, or a basic maths qualification.

You might think that this sounds like a full- or part-time job, but I think it equally stacks up as a side hustle due to the fact many people and/or businesses out there only need support for a couple of hours a week. A lot of entry-level VAs simply need a computer, phone and access to the internet, plus some basic software such as Microsoft365. This is all you'd need to work for me, but client needs will vary, and the more skilled VA roles will require a lot more, so check before you accept a role.

There are loads of sites you can join to become a VA. Or, alternatively, you can advertise on your social media channels or any flexible working forums you may be a part of. The money you can make depends on experience, but average rates start from £15 per hour up to £30 and beyond.

Similar to VA work is:

Transcribing
If you have a good ear and fast fingers, then this could be a fantastic way to make some extra cash in your spare time, as you can charge between £15 to £25 per hour.

Social media manager
Having an engaging social media presence is crucial for many businesses and, indeed, individuals, but this takes time, knowledge and effort. So, if you love the digital landscape and know how to create bespoke content which captures an audience, offering this skill can be a real asset and earn you anything from £17.50 per hour upwards.

Even more side hustles...

We've discussed specific sites that can help you achieve your moonlighting for money goals. Now we're going to look at some others that can help secure you side hustles across a broad range of activities:

Airtasker

To become a 'tasker', you set up a profile on this platform which highlights all your specific skills and attributes. Then all you need to do is search through the posted tasks to offer your skills for a job.

The great thing about this site is that they have very clear price guides to make sure you are charging the right amount for specific roles. Also, the array of jobs on here is vast; one man got paid to blow up and then later deflate a large paddling pool during a hot spell.

Jobs include:

> General handy-person duties

> Deliveries

> Cleaning

> Design

> Admin

> Computers

> Research

> Promotions

And many more.

Using this platform also covers you as a 'tasker' under their general liability insurance.

Taskrabbit

This is another site for a broad array of roles, including cleaning, flat-pack assembly, painting and gardening. There are also highly skilled tasks advertised, including plumbing and electrical, but you will obviously need to prove you have the right qualifications to undertake any of these. Taskrabbit is a national site that covers the country. They add an additional 15 per cent to the total amount billed plus a trust and support fee, which is all paid by the client.

Fiverr

This platform is specifically targeted to those of you who can offer digital services:

> Graphic design

> Writing content

> Translating

> Digital marketing

> Video editing

> Web design

> Creative writing

> Virtual assistants

> Digital illustration

All of these sites are great resources to secure quick side hustles and many offer multiple advantages but you can also choose to advertise and market your side hustles yourself:

Create a website
There are now lots of tools out there to help you create a website that is very cost effective. Including purchasing the domain name and hosting fees, you could be looking at as little as £3 a month, yet it will make your side hustle look so much more professional.

Utilise social media
You will need to create and manage a professional social media account that clearly showcases your brand and what you are offering to potential clients. Make your social media account a vibrant and engaging space for potential clients to engage with you. Populate it with loads of information, images, videos and make sure you keep it updated regularly.

Join forums, targeted social media groups and community pages
Most services will have forums and communities in which you should embed yourself to meet potential clients, see your competition and hear the needs of the community. These are great places in which to network – crucial if you want to have a long-running, money-making side hustle. Via these community pages you can chat with local business owners and set up in-person meetings to showcase them your offerings.

Getting your hustle off the ground
When starting a new side hustle it can be difficult to break

into the market. Here are some tips to develop your customer base:

> To get yourself started so that people review and share your details to their social and/or professional groups, offer first-time discounts and, depending on your hustle, think of ways you can reward loyalty with special offers.

> Customer care is king. You are only as successful as your reputation so you must ensure that you conduct yourself with the appropriate manner. Always be courteous, helpful and respond to questions or queries swiftly.

> Deal with any complaints head-on. Mistakes happen, we are all human, but don't get frustrated and respond inappropriately if someone has a complaint. Listen to it and ask for any supporting evidence so that you can dutifully investigate any issues.

As we've discovered, side hustles are a vast world where pretty much anything can make you some extra cash. I've given you some examples of proven and tested hustles that can work around your other life commitments and don't require a lot of time. Of course, you can turn any of these into a part-time or even full-time role, but what I wanted to show you is that there are ways to supplement your income quickly and effectively without losing all of your precious time. There are so many other side hustles to be found, so think about your skills, personal attributes and talents because I am confident you can turn them into tonnes of cash.

Before we move on to the next money-making activity, a little bit of important admin:

> Make sure you follow the law.

> Have in place any insurance legally required to perform your side hustle. If using a third-party site, they may cover your insurance but read the T&Cs to confirm this.

> Adhere to any local authority rules and regulations with regards to your activity.

> Comply with all health and safety regulations.

> Only perform side hustles you are experienced to do and have the right qualifications for where necessary.

> Make sure you know of any fees or costs that you will need to pay to a regulatory or governing body.

> Ensure you know how any supplementary income may affect the income tax you will need to pay. If you regularly sell goods or services earning over £1,000 a year, you will need to make HMRC aware as you will be deemed a 'trader'.

I know this might sound a little draconian but remember, I want you to make money, not lose it! Happy side hustling.

CAR BOOT FOR EXTRA LOOT

Some of my favourite memories from when I was a young boy are of going to car boot sales with my parents. If you're not that familiar with them, car boot sales – or, as most of us call them, car boots – are, in their simplest form, a place where people (not businesses) come together to sell household and garden items.

My parents would prepare and go to sell at car boots once a week – usually an assortment of second-hand items from around our home or deals they'd picked up. One of their ingenious ways to make money was out of cheap sweets and chocolates they could get from the local cash and carry but sell on for profit. I remember how most Saturday nights involved my mum weighing out various sweets to package up into white paper bags to sell on – I'd always sneak a wine gum for myself.

One of the less fun memories is of being woken at the crack of dawn to get to the car boot on time – what's that saying, the early bird catches the worm? Well, at car boots this is definitely true as they start and finish early. Anyway, I digress. Once woken, we would somehow all squeeze into our tiny car with all the goods we had prepared to sell that weekend. We'd drive to one of the many car boots around our local area and set up stall.

Car boot sales are definitely responsible for creating my first ever excitement for and engagement with selling interesting things to make some money. It was at car boots that I saw trading in its rawest form. Ordinary people from all walks of life coming together to create an arena of selling where their sole mission was to get the best price for their items, doing a battle with other sellers to make sure they had the upper hand and competitive pricing – it was exhilarating even for seven-year-old Dan, and I got so excited hoping we would sell everything but the paper sheets we used to display our items (though 40-year-old Dan would definitely sell those too).

This is also where I learnt from the greatest. Car boots were where I watched in awe as my mum was in her element. She balanced the greatest combination of charm and politeness with an unrivalled determination to sell and get the best price possible. Watching her within this arena influenced me from such a young age and planted the seed that when I grew up, I wanted to trade. I loved the hustle and bustle of an open commerce environment and fundamentally learnt within those long days at a car boot that you can make money whilst smiling, interacting and putting good energy into the world. This selling frenzy had such a lasting impression on me that I could even go as far to say I was born in Sheffield but forged at the car boot!

So, let's get to it . . . how do you sell at a car boot, what can you sell there and what are my tips and tricks to succeed?

Once you've absorbed all my guidance on this, you could quite literally pack up your car and start making money as soon as your reach your nearest car boot!

One of the most important things you need to consider is which car boot to set up your pitch at. Many people will suggest that you should travel to wealthy areas because of a misconception that this will secure you a greater return. I disagree. Car boots attract people from all socioeconomic backgrounds, so if you are at a reputable car boot with decent second-hand products to sell, all different people will travel to you (and, let's be honest, the wealthy ones can afford to travel further). It's also worth mentioning that the further you have to travel, the more petrol you will use, which is eating away at your profits before you've even started selling.

I advise that you find a car boot within a 30-mile radius of your home. There are two sites that I use which really help to identify the best location for you and your items. Both www.carbootjunction.com and www.findcarboot.co.uk are great research tools to tell you about various car boots in your area with loads of additional information about opening times, entry fees, days and months of operation and whether you can book your pitch in advance – which I would always suggest as it isn't uncommon for you to be turned away if a car boot is over subscribed.

Once you have shortlisted a couple of local car boots, go and recce them. This is a vital part of your preparation which will teach you if it attracts the type of people who will buy your goods and how many buyers and sellers attend; it's also an opportunity for you to see where you want to pitch your stall.

As with which car boot to choose, I also disagree with the

consensus of where you should pitch up – I promise I'm not usually this disputatious, but I really want to help you make the most money. Many will advise you to pitch as close to the entrance or exit as possible, but I personally think about halfway in, ideally near a food stall, is the absolute sweet spot. At the entrance, people are inquisitive but haven't seen enough to judge whether you are a good deal or not; at the end, you risk buyers having no funds left. In the middle and near a food truck, buyers have eased into the car boot, their purse strings are loosened, they have sussed out the general offerings and are ready to start spending (plus food trucks/stalls always attract the greatest footfall). If you can pre-book your pitch, your recce will help you identify which area you want to book and even if you can't pre-book, you can at least ask for this spot when you arrive on the day.

During your recce, you will be able to identify what sells best, whether there is a theme or trend to this specific car boot and if that aligns with what you will be offering. On top of this, a recce will help you to understand the choreography of a car boot. If you're new to them, they can be daunting and a little overwhelming, so your recce will give you a sense of the mechanics of how it works, how people interact and the art of the barter (time to witness Chapter 4 in action and an opportunity for you to practise your new skills).

With your site picked and the recce complete, it's time to prepare for your car boot sale. One of the most important things to do is to prep the night before – generally car boots start early (unless you're in swanky London . . . this will make sense at the end of the chapter) and often (not always) sellers can set up even earlier, before the gates open to buyers. So have everything prepared and put into piles ready to go straight into the boot the following morning.

Remember, you will need to pack in reverse order, as the last thing into your boot will be the first thing out. With this in mind, whether using a trestle table or rug to display your items, put this in last so that you can set it up first. If you are selling various items, I suggest putting them into categories so that you can display them efficiently and clearly as soon as they are out of the boot. Below is a diagram of how I suggest to best set up your stall.

ON YOUR TRESTLE TABLE

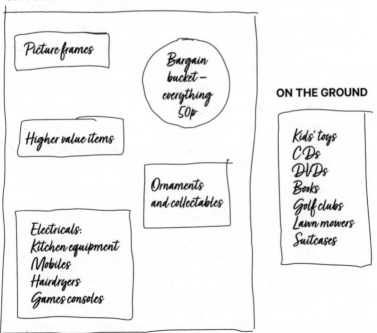

You'll need to be fast setting up if the car boot you are attending lets buyers in the same time as sellers. Even if you are allowed to set up earlier, some car boots give buyers the option to pay extra to get in at the same time as you, which means bargain hunters will be quick to pick through your offerings. So this preparation is vital to help you get your stall set up and in order before anyone can disturb it and cause you any unnecessary stress.

Make sure you use the night before to bubble wrap or box up any fragile items as there is nothing worse than getting to your location and finding some of your key items broken and unable to be sold.

Finally, if it is safe to do so and your car/vehicle is going to be in a secure location overnight, I'd suggest loading it the night before too. This means that when your alarm goes off at the unsightly hour (let's not fool ourselves, it is earlier than any of us want to be out of bed) in the morning, all you need to do is wash, get dressed and jump in the car!

One of the most common mistakes I see people making at car boots is that they forget the essentials. Car boots can be long and demand a lot of energy and attention, so make sure you have everything you will need for a successful sales day.

Below is my list of must-haves to enable you for a rewarding car booty:

> **Carrier bags:** Sounds daft but being able to offer people carrier bags may just snatch you a sale. If people have their hands full, a carrier bag or two might make them buy more. Let's be honest, we all have a bag for life storing hundreds of bags for life at home, so put them to good use.

> **Cash denominations:** You can get in a pickle pretty

quickly if you don't have enough cash to trade. Either start saving various denominations early or make sure you schedule enough time to go to your bank, a post office or a local shop to secure these in advance. It's better to have too much than too little – let's face it, you don't want to be undercutting your prices because you don't have the change to offer:

- 15 × £1 coins

- 16 × 50p

- 40 × 20p

- 40 × 10p

- Lots of 5p pieces and pennies (and any notes you may have).

> **Food and drink:** Armies march on their stomachs and, similarly, sellers will only succeed with a full tummy! Don't make the mistake of parting with your profits to line a food stall's pockets – remember, it's great to support local but there are plenty of people coming to spend their money; today, you need to make your money. So pre-make some sandwiches, pack some snacks and have flasks of tea, coffee and plenty of water in your car to keep you fuelled for a busy day of selling.

> **Coats, covers and chairs:** Aah, the great British weather. We all know that we can have a balmy winter and a freezing summer so pack clothes for all seasons. Also, pick up some cheap transparent dust sheets to cover your stall if the weather turns, as hardy car booties will stay to try to pick up a bargain

regardless of the weather. Finally, a couple of foldable chairs will come in handy for some leg and foot relief – it's a long and hard day so don't let tired limbs cut short your selling window.

> **Plan your route:** Don't rely solely on a sat nav to get you from home to the car boot location – I can't begin to tell you how many times I've missed a turning even when following a sat nav. You may not be as bad with directions as I am but it's always handy to plan your route in advance so that you can be first at the location ready to set up your pitch and greet the early treasures hunters.

> **All the gear to make you a car boot pioneer!** Whether you invest or borrow these items, it is worth planning your pitch to make yourself stand out and your items appealing. Grab a trestle table from a local DIY store (it's a worthwhile investment), a clothes rail, a ground sheet and a mirror. These four items will help you to establish an eye-catching pitch – hang all the clothes on the rail so it's easy for buyers to look through and the mirror helps them to see how great they would look in them. You can arrange your second-hand household items on the trestle table and the ground sheet can hold bigger items or overspill that won't fit on the table.

> **The price must be right:** There is an age-old debate about whether you price up your items or not. Those who price up their items say it helps with buyers who may not want to ask; those who don't say it's because it can scare people off. I personally devised a little colour coding system which does both. You

set a price range for each colour so people will know the rough cost of each item – you'll start the negotiation at the high end of the price range, the buyer will start at the low end and hopefully you'll meet at a satisfactory point for both of you.

- Red: up to 50p

- Green: 50p–£1

- Blue: £1–£3

- Orange: £3–£6

- Purple: £6–£10

- Pink: £10 plus

You might also want to explore doing bundles. Create clear areas on your display with signs like 'everything in this box £1 each' etc. This helps create curiosity and gets people hunting for a bargain.

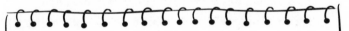

Dan's Top Tip

You'll achieve your higher prices in the morning when everyone is bright eyed and bushy tailed. As the end of the sale draws near and the crowds begin to disperse, allow yourself to reduce your prices to clear your haul.

Getting your pricing right is vital to succeed. Too high and people won't engage, too cheap and you risk not making a profit after your set-up costs are deducted. Like always, research is your friend and ally. Especially with expensive items. Look what other places are selling them for and monitor how quickly they are being snapped up. This will guide you on setting your prices. With lower cost items, aim for 10–20 per cent of the original RRP. Always remember that car boot buyers are professional bargain hunters, so your original pricing also needs to factor in the likelihood that you will be bartered down to a lower price.

> **Bring along a car booty buddy:** Doubling the manpower will ensure that you can engage with the maximum number of buyers quickly and efficiently. Split your pitch – one of you looks solely after the left-hand side, the other the right. People won't stick around for you to finish serving someone else, so this strategy can really benefit your profits. Make sure your buddy is confident to barter, charismatic and understands your pricing strategy.

> **Protect your pitch:** Unfortunately, car boots can attract people who may want to steal from your stall or even your vehicle. So, with your car boot buddy, you can best protect your items and yourselves. Car boots are wonderful because of the sheer scale of them and the frantic atmosphere of trading but this makes it difficult to concentrate and keep across everything.

Remember to:

• Keep your car locked.

• Have cash in a secure place, like a concealed money belt.

- Keep your car keys attached to you or in a zipped pocket.

- Always have your personal valuables on you: bank cards, mobiles, jewellery etc.

- Watch over slippery fingers searching through your stall.

> **The early bird catches the worm:** I don't mean to sound like a broken record, but it is vital to get there early, especially if you can't pre-book your pitch. If you arrive an hour earlier than the advertised start time, you're more likely to secure a decent spot and have the time to set up a great pitch that will attract the bargain hunters. I appreciate that car boots are early starts regardless, but having this additional time will make you more money. I reckon that the most lucrative deals happen within the first 90 minutes of setting up your pitch, so it's worth sacrificing a little sleep to secure those sales.

> **Pretty pitches:** Use my display guide from earlier to help achieve the best possible layout. You want as many eyes on your pitch as possible and you therefore need your items to be clearly visible. Categorising items is a surefire way for people to navigate your stall. I also have a rather cheeky tip which is to put children's toys on the ground sheet. Sometimes because they are bulky but mainly because I am unashamedly trying to entice children to my stall so that they pull their parents and guardians with them. Have a bargain bucket of items for 50p which will help draw people in;

hopefully, then they'll look at the more expensive items you may have. I keep all the most valuable items nearest myself. The broader you can make your stall, the more likely you are to make a sale. By having kitchenware, ornaments, toys, clothes, sports equipment and computer games you will attract someone with a specific need, but then they'll also be enticed to make a secondary purchase of another item. Get creative: using signs can make your stall more engaging and going the extra mile by having a tablecloth on your trestle table could put you a step ahead of your competition.

> **Pearly whites for a profit:** Did you know that a smile can deliver the big bucks? I've told you already about the age-old saying that we buy from people we like and it really is true. So, slap on a smile and be engaging from the outset. Don't get annoyed or angry when a seasoned car boot pro starts to haggle with you; they're not insulting your goods, they are merely trying to secure a bargain. Compliment potential buyers. If they are looking at clothes, tell them how well the colour suits them and ask them where they'd wear the item to open up a discussion. Remember to be engaging and present but not overzealous – how many times have you left a shop because the sales assistant is too full on? Or because they didn't seem to care? You need to find that sweet middle spot that shows the buyer you care and are listening but aren't being forceful.

Dress well, too. I'm not suggesting putting on your Sunday best, but I also don't want to see you in a string vest with ripped up shorts. Having a clean outfit that looks presentable tells buyers you look after yourself and therefore are more likely to have looked after the items you are trying to sell.

One secret weapon I often deploy to make a profit is having a tin of sweets with me that I offer up when people are browsing. Not only does this automatically disarm people but it will easily engage you both in conversation, break down any walls and potentially bag you a sale.

> **Waste not, want not:** Hopefully you aren't going to be a one-time car booter, but also you cannot guarantee the buyers coming to any specific sale. So don't throw away the remaining items left at the end of the day. Instead, pack them up for your next car boot sale. It's always worth another roll of the dice and if after a couple of attempts certain items still aren't selling, donate them to a charity shop instead of throwing them away.

> **Rules and regulations:** Car boots are serious business and each site will have their own set of rules and regulations, so please read through any literature or areas on the website to familiarise yourself with how to sell respectfully at each car boot. Generally we can assume:

  • Do not sell any illegal, counterfeit or items that need special licences, like drugs, alcohol, pornography and fireworks.

  • You will have a specific area where you can set up your stall, so understand the dimensions and check you aren't bringing display tables which won't fit.

  • Take away all your rubbish.

The main point is to have fun – this is what car boots are all about. A meeting of similarly minded people, creating a community where you can safely trade. But how much money can you really make, I hear you ask? Well, this is a difficult one to quantify because there are so many variable factors. How many items are you selling, what is the quality of your items, how much does it cost to participate in the car boot you've chosen and what are the costs to get there, etc.?

You can earn anything from £100 to £700 at a car boot but, as with all businesses, markets vary and you could make less one week and more the next.

One thing I do urge you to do in the first instance is plan and use my handy checklist to make sure you are working out profit after costs. Lots of people make the mistake of not including mileage and other factors when working out their profit – anything you had to fund to be able to sell at the car boot needs to be accounted for to work out your true earnings.

CAR BOOT SALE COSTS – CHECKLIST

What do you need?	Costs
Trestle tables	£25
Display Plinths	£15
Transport	
Drive 12 miles	£6 (50p per mile)
Venue fees	
Pitch fee	£7 (average pitch fee ranges from £6 – £12)
Total:	£53

Remember, investments in trestle tables and things you use to display the items you are selling are long term and you can spread the cost of these over multiple car boots to balance your profit and loss forecasts (but only spend on this outlay if you are planning to be a regular car booter).

Now you know the basics, let's take a look at what items sell well at a car boot.

In theory, you can pretty much sell anything and everything at a car boot – one man's trash is another man's treasure, so the saying goes – but you need to be sales smart with your approach, which means having a targeted strategy. By this I mean, selling items that have the broadest appeal for an impressive mark-up achievable in the least amount of your time.

There are three fundamental categories of people who attend a car boot:

> **The Bargain Hunters:** They are thirsty for items as cheaply as possible. They're looking for toys, tea towels, homeware and anything they can grab for a steal.

> **The Upcyclers:** These are the fabulous sustainability warriors who want to reuse and repurpose old household items. They're likely looking for lamps, tables and chairs that they can makeover into a sought-after item.

> **The Collectors:** This group is after your treasure. They want to find those rare items worth a lot of money that you haven't a clue about . . . so always remember my top tip:

Dan's Top Tip

Research, research, research . . . I know I say this A LOT but you have to know your items and their market value in order to make some well-deserved cash – I want you to line your pockets, not someone else's.

What to sell

Clothes

I don't think I have ever been to a car boot that hasn't had clothes for sale. Clothes sell like hot cakes, which is why you'd be wise to stock your car boot with plenty. I hope it goes without saying that there are some items you really shouldn't try to sell – I don't think anyone attending a car boot is interested in your old undies!

The main thing to remember is even if you don't love those clothes anymore, that doesn't mean that someone else won't, especially as the world moves to a trend of sustainable fashion.

A hot market for clothes is childrenswear. Anyone who is a parent will confirm how many clothes you need to raise your children and this gets very expensive, especially in the early years when, let's face it, the clothes are mainly catching something that's come out of your child's mouth or bottom.

A car boot isn't the place for your designer threads; we've

discussed previously how you can monetise these. The perfect sweet spot for a car boot clothes sale is high street that is in decent condition. Anything ripped or with faults will put off the majority of buyers and could even stop them from looking at your goods – just because people want a bargain at a car boot, doesn't mean they don't want decent quality.

Computer consoles and video games

The average house has about £800 of unwanted and unused technology sitting around gathering dust when it could be making you plenty of cash at the car boot. Generally, any generic computer console and mass-produced game can get you some pretty easy cash quickly, but there are also rarer items, so you really do want to follow my 'research, research, research' tip here. Before loading up your old tech into the car, check on generic resale sites the make and model of your console and if it has been discontinued. Discontinued can often mean nostalgic and when it comes to video games and consoles, and this can carry high price tags for you. Do the same with your unwanted games – anything limited edition or high in demand, could earn you more. Check back to Chapter 7 for more on this.

Jewellery

Costume and silver jewellery sell very well at car boots, but only costume and silver. Don't come armed with your finest gold – the international price for gold is so high that you will never achieve gold jewellery's full potential at a car boot. The same goes for precious stones (like diamonds). I always advise getting multiple valuations from various jewellers and pawnbrokers (at least four comparative prices) and to sell directly via this method.

If you are lucky enough to have any of the below costume jewellery brands, definitely don't sell these pieces at a car boot:

> Dior

> Chanel

> Weiss

> Eisenberg

> Trifari

> Else Schiaparelli

Always do you market research to check what brands sell best.

Silver sells really well at car boots, but make sure you check the authenticity before trying to sell it due to the fact that in the mid to late twentieth century, a lot of fake silver flooded the market, so we need to be sure your item isn't made of non-precious metals.

The following are easy ways for you to check the authenticity of your silver:

> **Hallmarks:** A UK hallmark certifies the standard of purity on silver (other countries have their own methods) so is one of the easiest ways to obtain authentication. Anything that starts with a country followed by 'silver' could potentially be fake as these are brand names not purity hallmarks (Mexico silver, Arizona silver, New Mexico silver, for instance). If a piece is stamped 925 or 999 (the most used purity marks but you can have 800 and 958) and has all of the following hallmarks, you can be confident you have silver:

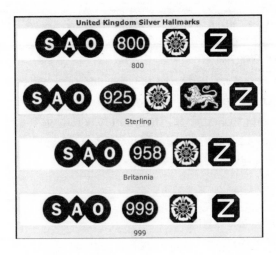

> **Tarnished silver:** Sterling silver will naturally tarnish over time because it reacts with sulphur in the air – and, interestingly, if you put your silver next to a boiled egg, it will tarnish even quicker. So, whilst tarnished silver may not look attractive, it's a good way for you to identify that it is real, unlike items you may have in your jewellery box that still look brand new, in which case they are more likely costume or non-precious metal pieces.

> **Run a magnet over it:** Real silver isn't magnetic, so if any of your 'silver' sticks to a magnet, I'm afraid it isn't the precious metal you were hoping for.

These are some of the easiest ways to check your silver. But remember, whilst tarnished silver is a good identifier for you, it'll sell better if you clean it up, so follow my next Top Tip before taking it out to market.

Dan's Top Tip

Get a bowl and put some foil in the bottom, add boiling water and sprinkle in baking powder. Immerse the silver for five minutes. Then, carefully remove it and almost all of the tarnish will have gone.

Children's toys

As with childrenswear, toys also sell very well for basically the same principle. As they grow, so does their brain and appetite for knowledge and learning. Toys are a great way for children to learn everything from the emotion of caring for a doll, to the strategy of a game at an older age or even language and numeracy skills.

To succeed at selling toys at a car boot, you need to make sure that the toy is in decent condition and has all the parts. Even if you don't have the original packaging, you can use my favourite tip and put all the parts in a clear bag, so the buyer can see they are getting everything they should. Most children's toys will sell well but my top list includes:

> Bikes – these are my star item and will definitely get you a return

> Board games

> Action figures

> Dolls

> Soft toys (these sell especially well if the tags are on)

> Lego – this is very popular

> Children's books

> Electrical toys

Baby items

I know we have covered childrenswear and toys, but baby equipment definitely deserves its own category, especially given the fact that nearly 600,000 babies are born a year in the UK.

My top baby items to sell are:

> Prams – another star item (I promise you, I don't have a thing for anything with wheels)

> Cots

> Baby clothes

> Baby shoes

> Car seats

Hobby Items

95 per cent of Brits say they have a hobby and hobby items can sell extremely well at car boots. These include but are by no means limited to:

> Golf clubs – these are my star item for this category

> Knitting equipment

> Sewing equipment

> Jigsaws

> ❯ Fishing equipment

> ❯ Sports equipment

> ❯ Musical instruments

> ❯ Gardening equipment

You never know if you are going to enjoy a new hobby, so by offering second-hand hobby items at your car boot you will attract lots of people who are keen to try but don't want the initial outlay of buying new.

Books

Despite the arrival of the eBook, physical books are still in high demand. Heck, you might have one in your hand right now . . .

In 2023, over 50 per cent of UK adults read a physical book, so they are still, and I hope will always be, in high demand. If your books are limited edition or had limited runs, check that you are pricing them accordingly and not selling too cheap.

Dan's Top Tip

When selling hobby items, create a sign saying something like 'hobby corner', as it will attract enthusiasts as well as people with an inquisitive mind.

Ornaments, furniture and home furnishings

We know that sustainability is here to stay and, like the cycles of fashion favourites, home furnishings also come in and out of fashion – kitsch is the current cool, so don't be afraid to drag out those old furnishings currently attracting nothing but dust in your attic or under your bed. Everyone at any age of their adult life will need furniture too, and the cheaper they can get it, the better.

Items to consider selling here include:

> Vases

> Pottery

> Paintings and prints

> Mirrors

> Light fittings

> Drawers and cupboards

> Bedside tables

> Tables

> Chairs

> Clocks

For anyone paying attention, you'll notice I didn't have a star item in this category, which is down to the fact that they all generally sell on a relatively even keel.

Kitchen items

Let's face it, there is pretty much a gadget to do everything for you in the kitchen, so these items are highly sought after, as many of us don't see the need to buy them new. Again, they need to be in a good working condition. Some highlights are:

> Kettles

> Toasters

> Electric mixers

> Weighing scales

> Measuring bowls

> Cake tins

> Storage containers

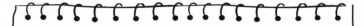

Dan's Top Tip

If the item is electric, it always helps if you can show it works . . .

Perfume and aftershave

Unopened bottles of perfume and aftershave go down a treat at a car boot but, surprisingly, even part-used bottles will still likely sell for a couple of quid. It's not going to pay for a holiday in the sun but if you don't like the smell, a couple of extra quid isn't to be sniffed at. Unopened gift packs of smelly treats and shower gels go down a storm too.

Music and DVDs

Streaming isn't for everyone and, just as for books, there are enthusiasts out there who love a physical item. Whilst this is not a huge money maker, they will still fly out of your boot – records, CDs, tapes and DVDs if priced at about £1–£2 will all sell well for you with minimal effort. If you have large stashes of these, try making your own curated box sets and themed selections to help drum up even more business.

Homemade treats

If you are a keen baker or cook, homemade cakes, jams, chutneys and spreads all go down well at a car boot. What better customer than the hungry bargain hunter who has been on their feet all day? Like some of the above, these aren't necessarily going to fund a romantic weekend away, but with some clever market research to price correctly, your delicious edible treats could still make you a healthy profit.

Whilst these are my top selling suggestions, you can generally try your hand with most household items at a car boot sale, but do steer clear of anything controversial or inhumane – books/DVDs from people who have subsequently been accused of anything untoward and animal items such as real fur and ivory are a no no.

Other things I would steer away from selling include personal items. I've seen people trying to sell lockets and photo frames with pictures of family member in them. Unfortunately, this will put off many customers. Anything which is engraved or overly personalised will also struggle.

Lastly, do think about the seasons. If you are holding a car boot sale in June, your big woolly coats and jumpers won't bode well. Unlike retail shops that may start to successfully sell autumn and winter items a month or so in advance, the savvy car bootie isn't coming to specifically fill a need, they are coming to find a bargain. If it's raining, you'll clean up with umbrellas; if it's hot, shorts and t-shirts will secure you a decent loot.

Don't forget, you can also trade at a car boot to pick up your own bargains too, so always keep your eyes peeled.

Before you move on, I've listed an array of my favourite go-to car boots from across the country, so take a look and get booked in. I promise you – you'll have a great time.

London

> Battersea. Known as 'the original car boot sale in London' it doesn't start until midday – how civilised!

> Wimbledon. With over 2,000 pitches this site is huge! You can sell everything here and people travel from all around the country to attend, so expect big crowds.

Midlands

> Eboot at Sutton Coldfield. This is a Friday car boot. It's an early start at 6am so I would get there at 4am. Worth it though, I've always found it to have a great atmosphere.

The north east

> York racecourse. Once a week. It attracts big crowds and it's a lovely setting. Items seem to go for good money at this car boot.

> Skirlington. This is the biggest car boot in the county. It brings in big crowds as punters only have to pay 40p each and kids enter for free.

> Strawberry Fields. This Bridlington institution is a favourite of mine; in fact, I have many happy memories here. With over 2,000 pitches Strawberry Fields attracts the crowds!

The north west

> Corbridge. Located at Tynedale rugby club this has a loyal legion of fans. It's a tried and tested safe choice.

> Hexham (Auction Mart, Tyne Green). Lively and always busy. This runs until December so you can keep selling almost up to Christmas. Great for selling those unwanted Christmas decorations.

East

> Ardleigh car boot. This is billed as Colchester's original car boot. It's gained legendary status in the car boot world. Worth a visit for sure.

> Bizzy Boots, Peterborough. This consistently gets thumbs up from sellers and punters. Long established and well run.

The south west

> Lansdown. Huge and spread over two sites. It feels very family orientated and often has a bouncy castle.

> Bristol Sunday market and car boot. It has a lot of variety which secures a huge returning footfall.

Wales

> Sully Sports Club, Penarth. Crowds flock to pick up bargains here with fantastic views.

Scotland

> Errol Sunday Market, near Perth. Open 50 weeks a year. A family favourite that draws in big crowds

Northern Ireland

> Shorts Sports and Recreation Club car boot, Belfast. This car boot has quite a boutique feel to it and I like it for being less occupied but still a lovely all-rounder.

CAR BOOT SALE TO-DO LIST

☐ **Research potential car boots:** 1 month before

☐ **Big clear out:** 1 month before

☐ **Research prices:** 2 weeks before

☐ **See if you can book a pitch:** As early as possible

☐ **Check tables, ground sheets, covers and display items:** 1 week before

☐ **Collect change:** 1 week before

☐ **Do a reccy:** As soon as possible

☐ **Box up items:** A few days before

☐ **Put items in car:** 1 day before (if it is safe and secure to do so)

☐ **Make food:** 1 day before

☐ **Pack cold drinks, waterproofs and warm clothes. Make a hot flask:** On the day

I have given you everything you need to be a successful car booter. With an estimated 30,000 car boots across the country, you will be sure to find one that will meet your needs. And be prepared to make some serious money; the popularity of car boots brings in roughly £1.5 billion nation-wide, so it's big business and has the potential to be very lucrative. It's easy and fun to do, and on top of making you cash, it will also declutter your home.

UPCYCLE TO UP-SELL

Upcycling is an industry worth £160 billion per annum and last year alone the term was searched for online 3 million times. Further research shows us that around 44 per cent of the population have attempted it and that it has fast become one of the most popular hobbies to earn extra cash.

Many think that the process of turning something old and maybe a little dog-eared into something new is a twenty-first century revelation but it isn't. For thousands of years, we have been repurposing and reconditioning items. Whilst the phrase 'up-cycling' is attributed to mechanical engineer Reiner Pilz, in a 1994 architecture and antiques magazine *Salvo*, where it was stated, 'I call recycling down-cycling. What we need is up-cycling'. It was then popularised by entrepreneur Gunter Pauli in 1998, we can probably trace the idea of revitalising something old by giving it a new purpose all the way back to early humans, when this would have been a part of everyday life.

We can definitely see its roots within fashion in the

nineteenth century when, under the reign of Queen Victoria, couturier Elise Kreutzer was tasked with repurposing the queen's daughter-in-law's garments. In Japan, *kintsugi* is the art of repairing broken pottery and using salvaged fabric to make quilts is a part of Amish culture.

Most notably, during the Second World War, we saw the creation of the 'Make Do and Mend' campaign. The British announced clothing rationing, so everyone was encouraged to upcycle their clothing to make what they already had last longer. By the 1950s, the term 'junk art' had been coined, which saw artists using waste materials to create art mainly from scrap metal. This continued through the decades, whether in the form of the trend to 'customise' in the 1970s and 1980s, or Maison Martin Margiela's 2001 collection featuring a gilet made from upcycled leather gloves. Nowadays, the art of upcycling spans many materials and, on top of the fact you can make money from it, it is a really sustainable way to reuse and repurpose, which addresses the growing concerns surrounding climate change.

When I married my husband in June 2023, we really wanted to have something for our wedding that would become a piece of our daily life. We asked one of our friends, a former TV exec and now a carpenter and avid upcycler, if we could commission her to make us something for our wedding day. She was super excited straight away and, through discussions, the idea developed that we wanted her to upcycle an old desk into our altar, which would then go into our home as a piece of furniture we would use and treasure for the rest of our days. It was really important to us that we repurposed something old (you know about my obsession with history!) and added some touches so it was in keeping with our taste but also to make it stronger to last us a lifetime – we were signing the register on this piece of furniture that was to make us a legally married couple, so it needed to bear weight.

She sourced an old 1920s desk (we love art deco) which was on its last legs, quite literally, and we discussed her ideas of how she would make it our perfect altar. What was a tired but wonderfully historical item, that I am sure could tell many a story, soon become this modern piece of furniture with regal blues and gold detailing. Brand new handles and strengthened side support means that it will last us decades and, whilst originally a desk, it sits proudly in our living room as a sideboard. We are in love with the end product and it's a fantastic example of how you can make money by turning an old item into something special that means a lot to someone.

Upcycling really inspires you to utilise every item you might have in your home and repurpose it into something new. Within *Money Maker*, we have discussed how to sell unwanted items from within your bubble but what about upcycling items that you have to give them a higher value, creating something that others can love and making you some serious cash? Or items that you can purchase for a little to make a lot . . .

You could be thinking that upcycling isn't for everyone. Some of us aren't blessed with the talents of a DIY legend and therefore throw the towel in before even trying. But I say – what do you have to lose? There is money to be made in old, unused items that you could give a new lease of life. The worst that could happen is that you try to upcycle something which doesn't go to plan but even so, I'm sure you could then sell it at a car boot.

Plus you have a world of inspiration at your fingertips that can really get you motivated. Social media has so many uses and one of the best is keeping up with the latest trends. Whether on Instagram or TikTok, you will find people who are amazing upcyclers and they document what they do. Keeping an overview of the social trends will help to direct you to the type of upcycling that is not only garnering attention but indicates the type of item people will buy.

There are so many people on Instagram doing wonderful things with upcycling and below are a few of the accounts I love:

@upcyclethat
@joannecondon
@the_shoestring_home
@maxreestore
@sixat21
@recyclemecreations

TikTok is a dangerous hole to fall into when it comes to upcycling as once you've engaged with one video, you'll soon find the next, and the next, and before you know it, you've lost hours! My husband makes a wonderful Channel 4 show called *Chateau DIY* and he often tells me the art of that show is transformation and seeing what talented people have done to create something with a brand new purpose. Well, I find it so engaging and whilst researching this book I have lost hours on the below TikTok accounts:

@studio_adash
@thefliphut
@rediscoveredbydanielle
@rickyrenovates
@ebonybasten

Find inspiration from accounts on social media, books on upcycling (there are plenty), general things in life that interest you and, before you know it, you'll have a clear idea of how you can enter the upcyling market and make money from what can be a really therapeutic activity.

To get started, I suggest not going too complex or overly ambitious. If you are new to the upcyling world, dip your toe in first – you can dive at a later date. Ideally, you have something within your home that is unused which you can transform into something new and sellable. But if you don't have anything (which I strongly don't believe – go back and put your home through a sieve), you can try sourcing something for free from any of the following sites:

> Freecycle

> ilovefreegle

> trashnothing

These are sites specifically set up to keep things out of landfill, but a lot of other sites we have covered in the book also advertise items that people want to get rid of for free. On some, you can even advertise what you are looking for:

> Gumtree freebies and regular Gumtree

> Facebook Marketplace and forums

> Preloved and their section called Freeloved

> Next door

> Shpock

> Freeads

As this becomes more and more of a money-making avenue for you, you can also consider going to car boots or charity shops and parting with a little of your cash to invest in something that can make you much more money. I even know of some people who have befriended workers at their local dump to bag a gem of an item that can be upcycled and sold on for good money.

In 2021, 118118money.com compiled a list of the five most popular upcycling items and the profit they can make you, using specific examples. This is clearly a couple of years ago so prices will have risen, especially with inflation, but I think it's interesting to observe what the market wants from these case studies:

1. **Upcycled cupboard.** With a cost of around £28 to sand, prime, paint and then varnish this into something new, you could retail for a profit of a staggering £347.

2. **Upcycled table.** If your painting and varnishing costs are £55, you could make a profit of £268.

3. **Upcycled bag.** Depending on the brand and style of bag, you could be looking at hundreds of pounds of profit when upcycling these items but even an ordinary bag, with an outlay of roughly £80 for sewing essentials, could make you a profit of £248.

4. **Upcycled light.** There is a huge demand for unique lighting and if you amalgamate an old bottle with a piece of wood to create a light, the costs are around £14, making a potential profit of £234.

5. **Upcycled chairs.** To oil, paint and wax an old chair will cost you roughly £46, so you could make a profit of about £173.

All these figures were calculated based on you having the main item to begin with. If you need to purchase the item, your profit margin will change, but as long as you are making a profit and covering your time at a value of minimum wage or higher, I think it's worth it.

Remember, anything can be upcycled and repurposed into something of value – not just furniture, but fashion, packaging, objects and even technology. We know our homes are treasure troves so take a look around to see what you could give a new lease of life whilst also making its value more than it is currently worth.

As a professional jeweller, I have come across some genius new creations using silver cutlery – wonderful bangles, rings and pendants – that all sell really well. We've discussed how fashion may have been one of the earliest sightings of upcyling, so if you have items that you can't sell for a profit in their current state, what could you do with them to give them a new purpose and a sellable value? I don't know how long it has been around but often when I visit antique fairs, I see old items such as military guns or fishing rods transformed into lights, which I find an ingenious way to upcycle and make an item that will create a brilliant talking point in a home. The opportunities are endless, and often the more creative you are with your upcycling the more money can be made.

I have met many people who have managed to transform their passion for upcycling into a full-time job that makes them plenty of cash, so it really is worth the effort to see if this could unlock you money-making potential.

We know that almost anything can be upcycled, so below are a few more of my ideas to get your creativity flowing and help make a passion into a money-making adventure.

Cabinets

Take something like an unused cabinet and transform it into an eye-catching display case. Use some sugar soap to give it a good clean, sand down any areas to get rid of old paint and flaws. Then paint it a bold new colour and try using some peel-and-stick wallpaper to create a colourful linings for the cabinet. Measure the space at the back of the cabinet you want to cover, cut this out on your wallpaper and simply stick it to the case for a phenomenal transformation.

Old wooden pallets

Pallets are a great material to upcycle. If you don't have any at home, often a DIY store or builder's yard will give you some for free. Why not attach some antique castors, repaint them in your favourite colour and, in no time at all, you can have a portable coffee or side table?

Notice boards

Whether you use old chopping boards or doors from broken cabinets, a flat piece of wood can be a quick and easy project to turn a profit. Give it a clean and apply some chalkboard paint to efficiently give this old material a new lease of life.

Stationery tins or flowerpots

Everyday items really can make you some money. Take some old food cans, thoroughly rinse and clean them, then file down any sharp edges. Find some unused wrapping paper around the house with an interesting design, cut it to fully wrap around the can and you've got pretty pen pots or flowerpots you can sell on.

Candle in a cup

The sky is the limit when it comes to your upcycling creativity and one thing that sells remarkably well is candles. So why not make some interesting and bespoke candles to raise some extra cash. If you have any old teacup and saucers, these can be the perfect receptacle. Get some candle wax and wicks to fix inside the old teacups so that you can sell candles in a cup.

Jewellery

What about using gems from around your home and turning them into costume jewellery? Pendants from old lights, beads from old clothing . . . Search around for beautifully shaped, colourful gems that could easily be made into a necklace or bracelet.

Handmade cards

These are wonderful to receive. Eleanor who works for me produces some amazing ones. She bulk buys postcards from around the world and turns them in to greeting cards, which is a really unique and bespoke thing to do. What do you have that could help you to create some stylised one-of-a-kind greeting card? You could go the extra mile and offer a customised service where you personalise the card with names and messages.

Whatever it is you decide to turn into your first upcycling project, the best way to succeed is by planning and preparing. Think through all the materials you need and pool them all together from around your home, making sure you have all the necessary tools. If you need additional tools, before you spend any money, check with family and friends who may be able to lend them to you instead. Remember, there are millions of unused tools lying around in people's homes and sheds, so the likelihood is that you'll be able to borrow what you need to keep your overheads down. If in the unlikely event you can't find a tool you need, explore renting one before going to the expense of buying it, unless you can see a use for it for the long term which will cover the initial outlay and continue to help you make money.

Next, you want to set aside an area where you will work. I find this a really helpful way to train your brain that when you are upcycling you are engaged in a money-making activity. Having a specific area set aside to do this work helps reinforce the idea that it is paid work. Make sure your space is large enough to cope with whatever size project you may undertake.

As you will have seen, all the accounts I mention to get inspired by have a clear brand identity – you quickly see what they are about, what they do and what the end product is like. It's imperative that with any money-making venture you have a clear brand identity to really stand out in the marketplace. Don't be afraid to show your personality within your branding and work; have a creative style and the confidence to show the market exactly what they would get from you and your upcycled work.

Brand diversification can be the difference between doing OK and smashing it when it comes to upcycling and crafting. You have to remember that there are lots of us on the internet trying to be the next big name in this field, so you can't just rely upon your cards, for example, looking pretty – what makes them stand out, what is different about them, what's your USP?

You need to put some serious time into thinking about

who your core demographic will be. It might sound unusual but try and envisage them as a person. What do they do for a career? What sort of property do they live in? Are they likely to be single, dating or married? Do they have children? Thinking about all of these questions helps you understand where they might shop, the amount of money they are happy to part with and what items they could really benefit from having. Once you know this, it will not only inform your designs and production, but it will also improve your marketing and sales strategy to get more sold.

I scroll endlessly through upcyling videos, so if you are serious about this being a long-term money-making activity for you, then make sure you set up accounts to highlight your branding and get your content seen by the masses. Create Facebook, Instagram and TikTok accounts where your content can be shared. It'll take some effort and commitment to get your profile full of content, so take loads of pictures and clip up videos to populate all your social channels. Inject some personality into your videos to help your content stand out above other peoples and encourage viewers to share them.

Your social channels will also act as a direct-to-consumer platform for you to sell your content. As soon as you have active socials promoting your brand and what you make, people will start to enquire about buying it and will want to know about bespoke commissions. Plus, there are loads of other places where upcycled products sell really well:

> eBay

> Etsy

> Ruby Lane

> Facebook Marketplace

> Preloved

Don't forget about in-person sales opportunities too. There are loads of vintage markets where you could set up a stall. Or see if any of the boutique shops on your local high street accepts concessions. Could your local cafe show and market your upcycled products? I see so many artists do this now, so why not you? Or do any local cafes or businesses want to commission you to upcycle something for them at a discounted rate, but they'll advertise your work in their retail space thereafter? When speaking with local businesses about potentially stocking your products, also ask if you can put posters up or leave business cards. The key to building brands is to flood the market – make sure everyone knows who you are and what you are doing.

The key notion of upcycling is to not only give something a new purpose or use – this process should make it more economically valuable than it was. So be mindful when pricing your items. Before you start work on something you already own – an old cabinet, for instance – research how much cabinets retail for, then work out how much you will need to spend on additional materials plus the time it will take you to complete the project. If you don't already own it, there will of course be that extra cost too. Even if it's just the cost of picking it up from someone getting rid of it via Gumtree. As long as there is profit to be made and a clear demand in the market, you are onto a winner.

There is plenty of money to be made from unique and attractive upcycled items and I can't wait to see what you create.

FESTIVE FUNDS

Did you know that UK households spend a staggering £15.7 billion on Christmas festivities? According to the WorldRemit 2022 Cost of Christmas Study, many families around the world will spend 156 per cent of their monthly income on festive celebrations.

With purse strings stretched and expectations high, it's easy to see how we fall victim to maxing out our credit cards to create the perfect Christmas. Not a fun fact but a true one nonetheless: the average household will take four months to pay off their Christmas debt and in the last couple of years, credit card bills have risen from an average of £2,200 to over £3,000.

Now that you are on your way to be a bubble entrepreneur, I am going to teach you how to turn your Christmas from being very much in the red to well and truly in the black. I have an abundance of tips and tricks to help enable you to have the perfect festive period without having to scrimp and save. I want you to be relaxed for what can be one of the most joyful times of year, not stressed about increasing credit card bills and lack of funds.

There are numerous ways to make money throughout December, but if you're too tied up with no free time, I will also highlight how to make cash during the Christmas Hangover (the early months of the following year).

Before we can look at the best ways to get the money flowing in, I need you to create a realistic overview of what you expect to be coming in from your regular earnings and what you would ideally spend to create the best Christmas for you and your loved ones. Remember, lying here will only cost you in the long run. Be totally honest and upfront and I will be able to teach you how to achieve those goals.

On the next page is a Christmas budget planner to help you on your way to a brilliant holiday season. Add up all your usual monthly outgoings (just like you do for your P&L planning), so rent/mortgage, heating, travel, etc. Then add to this all the festive items that are going to cost you (I have suggested what they might be on my planner but adapt to your personal needs).

On the bottom of the planner you can write your incomings and then your desired outgoings. Subtract the outgoings from the incomings to show you the shortfall you need to cover the cost of the festive period.

Christmas Budget

Description	Budget	Spent	Notes
Gifts			
Wrapping			
Postage			
Cards			
Home decorations			
Tree			
Food			
Drinks			
Travel expenses			
Entertainment			
Party outfits			

December incomings	December outgoings	Balance needed for best Christmas

Now that we know the shortfall by deducting your out-goings from your incomings, we can look at the various ways to make up this difference and hopefully even earn you a few extra quid at the same time.

Making money in December can be relatively straight-forward due to the fact that it's the season when everyone expects to spend and when people are willing to spend that little bit more than usual. There are two main ways to bring in the cash over the festive period: selling your unwanted belongings and side hustles.

Unwanted gifts

We already know that us Brits have far more than we need, so rummaging through your storage and the back of cupboards can be a sure-fire way to make some additional income. Each year, 21 million people receive a gift they do not want and I can safely say that I am within this head-count. Further research from eBay found that 77 per cent of us have an unwanted gift still in its original packaging, which is great to drive up your price point and the attrac-tiveness of the item. Whilst you might see these items as undesirable, we all have different tastes so there will always be a buyer out there for them.

The five biggest categories of unwanted gifts are:

> Clothes – 25 per cent

> Cosmetics and fragrances – 17 per cent

> Household items – 17 per cent

> Music – 16 per cent

> Technology – 15 per cent

Where you try to sell these items all depends on what you have, but I personally think for unwanted gifts you're best off using a broad all-rounder like eBay.

Even if the item is in its original packaging, it will still be viewed as second hand, so you won't be able to price it at a shop's retail value, but you'll still be able to get a decent return. To work out your item's price point, do some research to see what the item is selling for in the shops, then take a look at similar items that have been used and selling as second hand. Put your price somewhere in between the two and you'll soon be shifting your unwanted gifts to make some decent money. With 70 per cent of all Christmas gift shopping being done in December, now is the perfect time for you to capitalise on this market opportunity, whilst also decluttering your home.

Jewellery

Another area that you can monetise to make more is your jewellery. I mean, who doesn't love to receive jewellery for Christmas? I know I do and my husband definitely does.

If you've got unworn jewellery sitting collecting dust in a jewellery box why not clean it up and sell it on? You can pay a couple of pounds to have jewellery professionally polished to get it's sparkle back but I find that soaking metal jewellery in boiling hot water with washing up liquid (costume and other jewellery in tepid water), running over it with a toothbrush and then a finishing polish with a duster can do just the job.

The quality of your jewellery will determine where best to sell it. If you have nice low-cost dress jewellery, places like Etsy are a good websites to investigate. If they are heirlooms or you know they cost a pretty penny, I would suggest pawnbrokers or jewellery stores. You can put high-value items into auction and set a minimum so that if they don't reach the value you would like, you can keep it and try again another time.

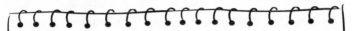

Dan's Top Tip

Don't confuse an insurance valuation with the market value of your item. Insurance valuations are higher because they have to cover the cost of replacing and potentially re-making a piece of jewellery. This takes time and money, so your insurance valuation will always be inflated and not a reflection of your item's true value.

Decorations

December is a pretty good time to sell unwanted Christmas decorations. Most people like to change colour schemes and how they decorate their homes every couple of years, if not every year. Whilst I don't have an official statistic about decorations, I am pretty sure UK households have enough tinsel to wrap around the world twice!

Dig any unwanted decorations out and start selling them on. This is not only great for your pocket but also the planet. eBay, local Christmas fairs and if you can find a car boot sale in December, are best places for you to sell at. You could even try contacting local businesses who are likely to be more inclined to purchase a second-hand artificial tree or nativity set for their decorating needs.

Clothes

I don't think there is ever a time of year when you can't sell clothes, but the party season of December is great to sell on fancy dress, anything party themed and all of your old Christmas sweaters. It's extremely extravagant, but I buy a new Christmas jumper each year so that it's a talking point in my pawnbrokers. Everyone loves a festive jumper, so much so that in 2021, £14 million pounds' worth of Christmas-themed jumpers were sold in the UK and that trend looks like it will increase for years to come. With parties taking place throughout the month, you could make hundreds selling your clothes in December, but you could also rent them if you don't want to part with them forever. Take a look back at Chapter 6 for my expert advice on renting out your wardrobe.

Festive side hustles

If you don't have valuable items to sell to raise extra cash for the festive period, why not take on a side hustle to make more money?

December is probably the month when the most people are time poor, which you can use to your advantage to offer services that help people achieve all they need to do for the festive period. With the convenience of social media, you can quickly and clearly advertise the products or services you are offering to raise the additional cash you need this month.

Some of my favourite side hustles are:

WFH (working from home)

You can literally make extra cash from the comfort of your couch. I've seen loads of fantastic and easy-to-navigate apps that you can download that have been created to specifically find workers for people with jobs they need done. Obviously, if you are working from home, these apps are aimed at people who can offer administrative services, tech support, social media management, marketing, design, etc. I recommend www.peopleperhour.com and www.fiver.com as really good sites for you to use if you have these sort of skills.

Dog walking

With time in such short supply and people needing to rush around to prepare for the festive period, there is never a better time to offer your services as a dog walker – especially as in the early 2020s we saw a 30 per cent uplift in the amount of people buying dogs. Depending on the area you live in, you can charge £10–£20 per dog, per hour. So if you could manage a couple of dogs at a time and have 40 hours a week to spare, you could earn up to £1,600 per week.

Christmas baking

The festive period is a perfect opportunity to put your baking skills to good use. With so many parties throughout the month, family, friends and local businesses will likely bite your arm off if you can supply them with sweet treats. Homemade Christmas cakes and puddings, Yule logs, gingerbread and truffles are just some of the sweet treats you can sell to supplement your income.

Make sure to cost up your ingredients, time and any packaging costs to work out how much to price your baking.

Dan's Top Tip

Well this one is less of a tip and more a legal requirement. If you plan to sell any perishable items you have made at home, you will need to check with your local authority about the regulations covering this, including whether or not you will need your kitchen registered and any other necessary requirements you have to meet.

Ensure you are making a profit, then use social media and networking to spread the word about your services and watch the orders come flowing in.

Babysitting

As it is the season to be jolly, there will be loads of local parents looking for babysitters so they can attend all the parties at this time of year. I suggest offering your services in your local area to people who know you and your family. This way, there will already be a level of trust and you'll probably already know the children so it will be easier for the parent(s) to be able to leave their little one(s) with you. Charging minimum wage is roughly the right amount for babysitting services but you can probably add a few extra quid to your hourly rate at this time of year.

Personal shopper

As we get closer to the big day, panic will be prolific across the country with forgotten presents, unexpected last-minute guests and slots of delivery services booked up. So there is a real opportunity to offer your services to meet the large demand. Whether grocery shopping or picking up gifts, you'll be able to charge a decent hourly rate for your time and help at this time of year – about £12–£15 per hour is a high enough rate to earn some decent money without it being too high to scare people off.

Make hampers

My little sister makes the best hampers for Christmas. Every year, each member of our family gets one and they feel so personal and unique, such a treat to receive – we love them. The great thing about hampers is that they don't require a huge amount of skill, so most of us could do it – though my sister's do look beautiful and I'm not sure I could quite match her creativity. Utilise your social media to advertise your festive hampers or even put up signs in local shops and businesses.

Obviously work out your costs for the items you'll include in your hampers, and the hamper or container itself, add on an hourly wage and you should be making a lovely profit whilst also offering a great product for this time of year. Utilise unwanted items from your home to form the foundations of your hampers and then you will only need to purchase a few additional items to complete them. I looked into a few options based on hampers my sister made and, as a guide, if additional items added cost £10, you could sell the hamper for £25, and if the additional items added cost £15, you could sell the hamper for £35. You can earn more depending on the produce and how bespoke you make each hamper.

For food hampers, I like to support local and independent businesses, so try to buy from local delicatessens, cheese makers and chocolatiers. December is the time of year when people are less likely to be watching their waistlines, so if you can offer homemade treats, they will make your hampers even more desirable. Things like jams, chutneys, homemade fudge, etc. will all go down a treat.

A good marketing ploy would be to theme your hampers. Say, 'Christmas extravaganza' for the ultimate Christmas hamper or 'Festive fuel' for a sweet treats hamper. There are so many options that can help you stand out. Don't get too over excited with your hampers: it's so easy to over buy/make but I find about ten items to each hamper is the perfect size.

How you set up your festive hamper hustle is entirely up to you. Some people can benefit from a lower cost outlay for a higher profit margin and bulk buy items, but, whilst it is more work, I prefer a more personal service utilising local suppliers. If you opt for this method, make up one hamper to use for marketing and promotion and then make the rest to order so that you don't end up with wasted stock and out-of-pocket expenses.

Remember, if you are selling hampers containing foods you have cooked in your own home then you may need to get your kitchen registered. Before you bake and package goods to sell, check with your local authority about any regulations in your area.

Finally, don't forget, festive hampers don't necessarily need to be food based; let your creativity flow and offer something unique. Below are a few ideas from me to get your started:

> Pet hampers

> Children's hampers (drawing books, colouring pens, etc.)

> Back to school stationary hampers for the New Year

> Quiz night hampers

> Movie night hampers

> Date night hampers

Gift wrapping

I don't know about you but my gift wrapping goes as far as putting a Christmas present into a bag and handing it over, so I would definitely pay for someone to do my wrapping for me. Offering to wrap people's Christmas presents is an easy way to make extra cash and, based on some of the presents I've received in the past, there are plenty of people out there who would benefit from this service.

You can either offer a wrapping only service where you charge an hourly rate or you could go further and offer this service with a selection of wrapping paper, bows, etc. which you provide.

To get yourself started, find a broad range of items of all shapes and sizes from around your house, then get various Christmas-themed wrapping and bows. Wrap all the items and take pictures to upload to your socials to advertise your service and prove how well you can do it – I would set up a bespoke page for this on social media and use your personal page to help promote it. People's tastes vary, so simple print wrapping will likely appeal to the broadest market. Try to use wrapping that is made of recycled paper.

You have to make sure that you cover any hard costs when thinking about your pricing. If you are just offering a wrapping service with your clients providing all the materials, offer a reasonable hourly rate, but if you are providing paper, ribbon, tags, etc. I would opt for a per item pricing strategy. Check the pricing of others in your area to make sure you're offering competitive pricing but as a general steer, I would suggest £4 for a small item, £6 for medium and £8 for large, or £15 per hour.

Offering a discount can always help secure more orders. According to coupon marketplace RetailMeNot, 80 per cent of people are more likely to try a new product or service if a discount is offered. You could make Wednesdays your midweek wrapping discount day and offer a 10 per cent discount on all services.

Seasonal temp work

As a business owner, I know only too well how hard it is to find decent temporary staff during the festive period. So if you have extra time to spare, there are plenty of companies looking for festive temp staff.

Some of the businesses that will definitely need additional staff at this time of year are:

> Delivery companies – if you have a driving licence, people like Amazon, Deliveroo, etc. will have higher demand than they can supply without temp workers at this time of year.

> Bar work – with Christmas parties throughout December and sometimes into January, you will definitely be able to get some temp work in the hospitality sector.

> Department stores – with greater footfall and more purchasing in December, plenty of shops and retail outlets will be crying out for extra help.

These are just a few of the money-making temp opportunities out there but there will be plenty of others. Take a look around your local area and keep an eye on businesses' social media accounts to see opportunities.

Whilst the traditional colour of Christmas may be red, I eagerly want you to enjoy the festive period with your bank balance in the black. So, find some items you can sell or get yourself a festive side hustle to cover the additional financial strain of this time.

ENDNOTE

Congratulations, you are now officially a Money Maker – welcome to the club.

There may not be pounds in your pocket just yet, but by reading this book, you have learnt all the skills you need to turn yourself into an empowered bubble entrepreneur.

I want to remind you that whilst the ever-changing economic landscape can often feel bleak and daunting, you now know how to fight back and use yourself and your belongings to raise more cash so that you don't just economically survive but can fiscally thrive.

Whether you start to moonlight for money, make wages from your wardrobe, find a jackpot in your hidden treasure or, as I strongly advise, follow as many of the chapters in this book to help raise more cash, you have the knowledge and the power to succeed.

You may have started this book with trepidation and caution, but now I hope you can see all the opportunities around you and that making money isn't the terrifying task people often believe it to be. Strip it all back to the basics; we all have something, whether a skill or an item, that will help someone else out. So put a price on it and start earning that extra cash you deserve for the things in life I want you to have.

However large or small, use what you have gathered from this book to make your dreams a reality. Once again, congratulations on becoming a Money Maker; this is only the beginning, and I cannot wait to hear all your success stories.

ACKNOWLEDGEMENTS

From Dan:

Thank you to my wonderful husband, Joff, the man who loves and supports me unconditionally, my soulmate. I can't quite believe the adventures we have been on and the ones coming up in our future. You persuaded me that my knowledge of how to make money could genuinely help others and that now was the time to put pen to paper – writing this book with you has been a joy beyond words.

To my mum, Queenie, your drive and ambition to constantly provide for our family has motivated me throughout my life. You taught me the importance of hard work and determination to succeed, plus how kindness and fairness are two principles we should follow in life, professionally and personally.

To my sister, Cherise, you supply love, support and advice in the bucket loads. I'm so proud of the wonderful woman and mother you have turned into.

Thank you to Teddy and Leo for always managing to put a smile on our faces; your Uncle Dan Dan and Uncle Joff love you very much.

Thank you, Dicky, my father-in-law, for your steadfast loyalty and guidance. I look forward to many more nights down at the Triangle chewing the fat over a pint or two. I am so proud to be a part of your family.

This book would not exist had it not been for a chance meeting in the *This Morning* green room with my fabulous literary agent, Rachel Mills. You trusted that I could write this book and have worked so hard to guide me throughout this process.

To the phenomenal team at Hodder Catalyst; Lauren Whelan, you wonderful bundle of energy – you understood what we wanted to get across in this book straight away and embraced our message. Thank you eternally for giving our book life! Thank you also to the fab Naomi for keeping us all on track, our super talented copy editor, Liz and our hotshot publicity/marketing duo, Becca and Janet. Big shout out to Antonia, Sarah, Briony and Matt – thank you for all your hard work.

To my amazing *This Morning* family. Thank you for welcoming me with open arms, I'm so lucky to work with such talented hosts. And to everyone behind the camera: Martin, Vivek, Daisy, Emma, Kerry, Juliet, Jess, Sarah and the Queen of the Green Room, Fleur. All of you and so many more have no idea how you have changed my life for the better and I am eternally grateful.

To my wonderful team, Ellie, Selwa, Julie and Amy, you are not only my colleagues but family and I'm lucky I get to work with such talent.

There are too many friends to name individually but we love you all dearly and appreciate everything you do for us.

Finally, thanks to Albert, our wonderful, slightly neurotic sausage dog, Colin, our deaf albino elderly cat and Pedwar, who's resting with the stars. We love your companionship.

From Joff:

This journey started with four words... 'I'll take you dancing', which were the first words I ever said to my now husband, Daniel Hatfield – he's Dan to you all but always Daniel to me. I never believed I would meet someone with the same level of ambition and curiosity in the world, and I am grateful beyond words not only that I get to share my life with you but that we co-wrote this book together to try and empower others. Thank you for being the exceptional man you are.

I want to thank my dad, Richard, who worked tirelessly to raise me and showed me that anything was possible with a bit of elbow grease and determination; you are an incredible role model, friend and parent. My siblings, Jill, Jamie and Chesney, I am so proud of what you have achieved, which inspires me daily. To all our nieces, nephews and godchildren, we love you and can't wait to watch you flourish.

To my dad's life partner Sheila and my biological mum, who are unfortunately no longer with us, you taught me that life isn't guaranteed and that we all need to go out there and make every day count. And Ann, who filled me with cheesy jacket potatoes and beans, making me the strong man I am today.

My amazing mother-in-law, Queenie, you are more like a best friend and your unwavering love, guidance and support keeps Daniel and I motivated and striving to be the best we can be.

Mark, Steve, Helen and all my amazing team at Spark Media, thank you for the wine, the theatre, the food and the reassurance that we could write this book.

Lauren and Naomi, thank you for being the driving force who championed us to make this book, Becca and Janet for helping us get the word out there, to our fabulous proof-reader Antonia, for our stunning jacket design from Sarah, beautiful design and typeset from Briony and production management by the talented Matt, and everyone else at Catalyst who has supported the creation of our very first publication – you guys are the best.

Liz, our phenomenal copy editor who kindly didn't laugh at our first manuscript and helped us make sense when words failed us.

Our amazing friends, who, regardless of our insane schedules and full-on work commitments, are always there to help us achieve our goals and raise a glass of fizz when we do.

Lastly, to all of you who have bought this book, we hope it gives you the skills to achieve whatever money-making dreams you have.

REFERENCES

1 Hannah, F. (2018). 'British inability to haggle could cost us £500 each year', *The Independent* [online], 28 Jul. Available at: https://www.independent.co.uk/money/spend-save/haggle-price-negotiate-lose-money-uk-savings-costs-british-a8464156.html [Accessed 18 Dec. 2023].

2 Drake, T. (2001). 'Kitchen Gadgets In British Homes', Tap Warehouse [online], 21 Jul. Available at: https://www.tapwarehouse.com/blog/latest-news/kitchen-gadgets-in-british-homes [Accessed 18 Dec. 2023].

3 Hannam, S. (2023). *'Brits urged to recycle millions of unwanted faddy kitchen appliances'*, AMDEA [online], [n.d.]. Available at: https://www.amdea.org.uk/brits-urged-to-recycle-millions-of-unwanted-faddy-kitchen-appliances/ [Accessed 18 Dec. 2023].

4 McLean, J. (2022). 'Dining rooms decline and orangeries on the rise', *Rightmove* [online], n.d. Available at: https://www.rightmove.co.uk/press-centre/dining-rooms-decline-and-orangeries-on-the-rise/ [Accessed 18 Dec. 2023].

5 Leathers, S. (2021). 'You could make £4,000 by renting out these items - how much cash is sitting in your attic', *Express.co.uk* [online], 9 Nov. Available at: https://www.express.co.uk/finance/personalfinance/1518648/make-money-homeware-items-renting [Accessed 18 Dec. 2023].

6 Strickson, W. (2021). 'Data suggests there could be 38 million unused bikes in UK', *Cyclist* [online], 12 Mar. Available at: https://www.cyclist.co.uk/news/data-suggests-there-could-be-38-million-unused-bikes-in-uk [Accessed 18 Dec. 2023].

7 giffgaff.com. (2022). 'Check Your Drawers', *giffgaff* [online], [n.d.]. Available at: https://www.giffgaff.com/hub/check-your-drawers/ [Accessed 18 Dec. 2023].

8 Jacques, L. (2022). 'Where are Brits Most Likely to Watch TV?', Bensons For Beds [online], 9 Nov. Available at: https://www.bensonsforbeds.co.uk/sleep-hub/where-are-brits-most-likely-to-watch-tv/ [Accessed 18 Dec. 2023].

9 Jacques, L. (2022).

10 Morris, S. (2019). 'The market for film memorabilia is worth £330m - could you make a mint?', *This Is Money* [online], 21 Aug. Available at: https://www.thisismoney.co.uk/money/investing/article-7376731/ [Accessed 18 Dec. 2023].

11 Boyle, M. and Pennarts, M. (2023). 'Side hustle statistics for 2023', Finder [online], 22 May. Available at: https://www.finder.com/uk/side-hustle-statistics. [Accessed 18 Dec. 2023].

12 Boyle, M. and Pennarts, M. (2023).

13 Boyle, M. and Pennarts, M. (2023).